D0181633

Creative Ministry

Creative Ministry

HENRI J. M. NOUWEN

Image Books

Doubleday

New York   London   Toronto   Sydney   Auckland

AN IMAGE BOOK

PUBLISHED BY DOUBLEDAY

a division of Random House, Inc.

IMAGE, DOUBLEDAY, and the portrayal of a deer drinking from a stream
are registered trademarks of Random House, Inc.

Book design by Chris Welch

The Library of Congress has cataloged the hardcover edition as follows:

Nouwen, Henri J. M.

Creative ministry

1. Pastoral theology. I. Title.

BV4011.N68 1971 73-139050

MARC

ISBN 0-385-12616-6

PRINTED IN THE UNITED STATES OF AMERICA

This Image Books Edition
December 2003

25   27   29   30   28   26   24

To Seward, Helen, and Anne Hiltner
in memory of
James Seward Hiltner

Preface to the New Edition

This new edition of *Creative Ministry* springs from collaboration among several parties who believe its message to be as relevant today as it was when Henri first published it in 1971. His core message is a call for ministers to look with "new glasses" at those they serve and to see the person in need not primarily as a problem but as a gift. Ministers then allow themselves to receive from and to let their ministry be shaped by the poor, who in the words of Saint Augustine are "the treasure of the Church."

This is indeed a creative vision of ministry and one that challenges each of us to open ourselves to the blessedness that Jesus recognizes in the poor. Written when Henri was teaching and lecturing in academic circles, this vision continued to inspire his vocational journey so that he ended his life living with and ministering primarily to people with disabilities and those who came to assist them. He said toward the end of his life, "I am convinced that this is the place from which I must live and minister. It is from my relationships here that Jesus inspires me to speak and to write."

I am grateful to Trace Murphy, Siobhan Dunn, and Joan Schadt at Doubleday for listening to suggestions about the revised text and for allowing time for the polishing of the original text. Maureen Wright at the Henri Nouwen Literary Centre in Toronto not only served as go-between for the publishers and editors but gave creative support to keep the task on the rails to completion. Finally, I am grateful to Sean Mulrooney, who did the major work of reediting the text to include more recent images and examples and to employ more inclusive language. He was precise and insightful, finding words that were faithful to the core message but relevant to the postmodern mind.

As collaborators, we hope that for you, the reader, Henri's words will continue to bear fruit in the lives of those who hear Good News through your unique and precious ministry.

Sue Mosteller
Literary Executrix of the
Henri Nouwen Estate
July 2003

Acknowledgments

This book would never have been started without the stimulation of the summer school students of the University of Notre Dame, who by their enthusiasm encouraged me to write and keep writing during six hot weeks, and who convinced me that spirituality can be discussed with a sense of humor. This book would never have been finished, however, without the honest and straightforward criticism of the Chicago priests, which made me rethink different issues and rewrite different chapters.

I owe much to the members of the Moreau Community for their hospitality, expressed not only by the offer of a quiet room in which to write but also by supportive friendship when writing did not seem very easy. I am especially thankful to Louis Putz for making me feel at home, to Jim Buckley for his constant help, and to Bob Antonelli for his personal interest, which made me beat the deadlines.

I also want to express my deep appreciation to Charles Sheedy and Jim Burtchaell for their invitation to give the lectures, to

Jack Egan and Don McNeill for their valuable suggestions for corrections, and to Betty Bartelme for her skillful help during the final stages of the manuscript.

I am very thankful to Rita Gorkowski and Carolyn Dalsgaard, who spent many hours typing and retyping the manuscript, and to Jeff Sobosan, who was so generous as to interrupt his own writing to reshape quite a few of my crooked sentences.

The Frank J. Lewis Foundation, sponsor of the pastoral theology program at the University of Notre Dame, offered the financial support for the preparation of this text.

I have dedicated this book to Seward Hiltner, teacher and friend, who introduced me into the field of pastoral theology; to his wife Helen and daughter Anne, who taught me much through their friendship and trust; and to his son James Seward, who made me realize that the length of life is less important than the intensity and sincerity with which it is lived.

H. N.

Contents

Jesus said to Simon Petrus:

When you were young
you put on your own belt
and walked where you liked;
but when you grow old
you will stretch your hands
and somebody else will put a belt round you
and take you where you would rather not go.

John 21:18

Creative Ministry

Beyond Professionalism

The main concern of this book is the relationship between professionalism and spirituality in the ministry. Since many very concrete experiences and events made my interest in this relationship grow, I would like to start with one of the cases that will illustrate the theme that runs through the following chapters.

One day during the past year a parish priest presented to a small group of pastors, of which I was a member, a report of his hospital visit to a twenty-six-year-old married woman who suffered from the fatal Hodgkins disease. The priest, a very intelligent pastor, was quite aware of the fact that this young woman would never leave the hospital and that she probably would die within the coming year. He brought the report of his pastoral visit to the group because he wanted to consult his fellow ministers about how to be of real help to his parishioner in the months ahead.

He described the young woman as a very happy, open person with a good sense of humor and full of energy. He wrote down parts of his conversation with her, word for word as far as he could remember, and concluded with the honest confession that he had felt extremely nervous during the visit and very uneasy and dissatisfied as he had left her alone in the ward.

When we studied this pastoral visit more closely, the conversation between the priest and his sick parishioner gave the impression of a long and painful attempt to avoid the reality that a very attractive young woman was soon going to die. They talked about the nurses, the food, the pains, the possibility of getting some sleep, and a great deal about how things would be later when she would be home again. It was obvious that the pastor himself was hardly aware of his avoiding the real issue; but in reading his own report over and over again, he discovered what really had taken place, and during the discussion with his colleagues it was possible for him to become aware that he probably could have been of more help to this woman if he had known a little more about pastoral care for a dying patient.

But then, somewhat surprisingly, one of the group members asked the priest, "Say—I wonder if you are really aware of the fact that *you* are going to die, too, perhaps not within a year but in any case pretty soon." Suddenly, all the discussions about skillful pastoral care stopped and there was a long silence. Then the priest said: "Perhaps not—perhaps I am more afraid to talk about death than my parishioner is, and perhaps I do not want her to remind me of my own mortality. . . ."

This response gave a dramatic shift to our "professional" discussion and made us more and more aware of the fact that those who want to be real ministers to a dying patient can never be so unless they are able to face their own death and relate in a Christian way to our undeniable reality. And it did not take long to realize that the question about ministry was intimately related to the question about the personal spiritual life of the minister.

This is only one of the many examples that have made me ask if spiritual guidance and professional formation in the ministry are not so closely related that any separation will, in the long run, do harm to both aspects of the daily life of the man or woman who wants to be of Christian service to brothers and sisters in the Church and beyond.

Perhaps we have to say that one of the main reasons for the many frustrations, pains, and disappointments in the life of numerous Christian ministers is rooted in the ever-growing separation between professionalism and spirituality. However, this separation is quite understandable if we look at the development of theological education during the last decade.

First of all, many seminaries have given up the routine of the spiritual exercises that structured the daily life of the student who wanted to prepare for the ministry. Daily hours of meditation, the recitations of long prayers, and regular services were often forced upon students as an essential condition for the saintly life at which they were asked to aim. Often it was suggested that only through this prayer-life could one be protected from the many dangers of the great world, and that no ministers would succeed in the long run if they were not faithful to what generations of ministers had found to be a support in their busy lives. But, when times changed and the life of the minister developed in new ways, it became less and less obvious how the many hours of piety were related to the daily concerns of the parish life. Ministers began to feel that prayer was more and more experienced as an escape into the safety of the interior life and a way of avoiding the burning issues that should stir the Christian conscience and be a challenge to engage in creative action. They would say: "Let us not close our eyes in order to indulge in nice and gratifying thoughts about God and his mysteries, but let us keep them open to the growing needs of the world around us. Why spend our time in rather dull and fruitless hours of meditation and contemplation when we could use our time better to train ourselves in the necessary skills and techniques that help us to be of real service to others?" It is no wonder that chapels became less popular places to visit and spiritual directors had fewer clients, and that, instead, much more attention was paid to supervised pastoral training in hospitals, prisons, parishes, and special city projects.

But there is another story, too, usually told by those ministers who for many years have been deeply immersed in the activities, worries, and concerns of the daily life of their congregations or neighborhoods. The multiformity of their work, the different forms of activities they became involved in, the great variety of persons they met, and the broad range of problems they touched finally made them wonder how they could live a unified life under such conditions and how their own most personal integrity could be maintained in the middle of so many contrasting stimuli. Many of these men and women have given so much of themselves in their daily, often very demanding, pastoral activities that they feel empty, exhausted, tired, and quite often disappointed. This fatigue strikes so hard because thanks are rarely expressed, progress is seldom obvious, and results are not often visible. Even when one knows how to be a good counselor and how to respond meaningfully to the needs of individuals and groups; even when one is fully prepared to be an agent of social change, the most burning question remains: "What moves me to do all this; where do I find the strength to find unity in all my diverse activities; how can I find the strength that helps me to be a person like Paul, who, in the middle of all his adventures, kept himself one through his unshakable faith in Christ and Him crucified?"

Going back to regular prayers? Spending more time with the reading of Scriptures? More meditation and hours of silence? Days of recollection? Retreats? Many have tried it but felt lost. It seemed as if they were saying: "If I cannot find God in the middle of my work—where my concerns and worries, pains, and joys are—it does not make sense to try in the hours set free at the periphery of my life. If my spiritual life cannot grow and deepen in the midst of my ministry, how will it ever grow on the edges?"

The question that seems to come up more and more in the circles of those who want to dedicate their lives to the Christian ministry is the one that lies beyond professionalism. There is hardly a doubt any longer that being a minister calls for careful preparation, not only in terms of the knowledge and understanding of God's word but also in terms of the ministerial relationships through which God's word comes to us. Just as a doctor, a psychologist, a psychiatrist, and a social worker need special skills to be of real help to their people, so a priest or minister will never become fruitful without the necessary training in the core functions of ministry, such as preaching, teaching, caring, organizing, and celebrating. Pastoral training centers have provided many priests and ministers with the necessary professional preparation and offered them many ways to make their work more satisfying, meaningful, and effective.

But although the main concern of ministers over the last years has been to find a place in the row of various helping professions, the question that is brought to their minds with an increasing urgency is: "What is there beyond professionalism—is ministry just another specialty in the many helping professions?" This question comes to the foreground again at a time when young students are questioning the value of the

complicated distinctions between academic disciplines and are
trying to come to terms with what is central and unifying in
their lives.

During the last few years, I have become overwhelmingly
impressed by the fact that priests, ministers, and theological
students who asked for supervision in their pastoral work are
asking questions that go far beyond their professional concerns. In the beginning, the emphasis quite often is on the best
technique, the most appropriate method, the most effective
approach: "How do I preach to a church congregation in a
language that will make me understood? How can I be of help
to a husband and wife struggling with marriage conflicts?
How do I assist a dying patient? How do I behave when my
community requires me to protest against the housing situation, wants me to work to alleviate poverty or fight segregation and social injustice? Should I remain nonviolent at all
cost, or is there a time when violence might be the only eth-
ical response?"

These questions are extremely important and call for intelligent discussions, careful research, and, often, long training
under competent supervision.

But these questions are not the last ones and not the most
decisive. Sometimes it even seems that underneath all these
concerns is the question about the spirituality of the man or
woman who raises them. Many students and trainees are
struggling with their own sense of being. Long before they
can ask themselves how to preach the Gospel to others, they
find themselves struggling with confusing questions: "Who is
God to me? Does Jesus Christ really motivate my life? How
do I think about my own life and death? What do I really have
to do with my neighbors? Is it my desire, task, or vocation to
intervene in anyone's life at all? Should I speak about love

when I question in my own heart that love is a possibility? Why read, talk, and teach about prayer when I never really experienced much of anything that deserves that title?"

These questions are not phrased in this very explicit way, but during the discussion of sermons, pastoral visits to sick people, religion classes, or any other ministerial task, I found that these questions are, knowingly or unknowingly, at the base of many frustrations for today's ministers. And if it is perhaps possible for a doctor to cure a patient even when the doctor hardly believes in the value of life, a Christian minister will never be able to be a minister if not rooted in a real, personal faith life that is the very core of pastoral ministry.

So, ministry and spirituality never can be separated. Ministry is not an eight-to-five job but primarily a way of life, which is for others to see and understand so that liberation can become a possibility.

There is today a great hunger for a new spirituality that is a new experience of God in our own lives. This experience is essential for every minister but cannot be found outside of the limits of ministry. It must be possible to find the seeds of this new spirituality right in the center of the Christian service. Prayer is not a preparation for work or an indispensable condition for effective ministry. Prayer is life; prayer and ministry are the same and can never be divorced. If they are, the minister becomes like an electrician or plumber and the priesthood nothing more than another way to soften the many pains of daily life.

If the desire for silence, for moments of contemplation and meditation, is not born out of our concerns for this world, we will soon become bored, not understanding why we have to be subjected to so many pious exercises. If God does not become more and more a living God to those who minister to the people of God every day, then God will not be found in the desert, the convent, or the silent hours, either. If professionalism is to be prevented from degenerating into a form of clerical manipulation, it has to be founded on the deep-rooted spiritual life of the minister as it develops out of the constant care for those to whom he ministers.

This is the main thrust of the following chapters. I hope to be able to show through the analysis of the five main functions of the ministry—teaching, preaching, individual pastoral care, organizing, and celebrating—the seeds of a spirituality for every man and woman who wants to be of service.

It will become clear that every Christian is a minister. The ordained ministry can be considered as a focus since the ordained minister gives the most visible shape to the different forms of Christian service. Therefore, the words "minister" and "priest" are often used in the following chapters. But what is true for ministers and priests in the formal sense is true for every man and woman who wants to live a life in the light of the Gospel of Jesus Christ. Therefore, in essence, this book is about the life-style of every Christian.

CHAPTER I

Beyond the Transference of Knowledge

Teaching

From a Violent to a Redemptive Way of Learning

Introduction

There was a time when God sent angels from Heaven with an urgent message for us. God still does. A few months ago, a Vietnamese Buddhist monk came to Holland and one day walked into the house where I lived. He was a thin man whom you would be afraid to touch. But his clear, fearless eyes radiated an insight so deeply impregnated with affection that the only thing you could hope for was understanding. While he looked straight into my eyes, he said: "There was a man on a horse galloping swiftly along the road. An old farmer standing in the fields, seeing him pass by, called out, 'Hey, rider, where are you going?' The rider turned around and shouted back, 'Don't ask me, just ask my horse!'"

The monk looked at me and said: "That is your condition. You are no longer master over your own destiny. You have lost control over the great powers that pull you forward toward an unknown direction. You have become a passive victim of an ongoing movement which you do not understand." It seemed as if he carved his message on my skin like a tattoo and then asked me to let it be seen wherever I go.

When we look at the situation of those who teach and

those who are taught, the same question comes to mind: Do teachers and students really know where their horses are going?

Students are men and women who are supposed to be in the exceptional situation that allows them to reflect on themselves and their society under the guidance of competent teachers. They have set aside a certain amount of time in their lives to look explicitly at their own condition, and at the condition of the world in which they live, in the hope of being better able to understand and act accordingly.

But when we realize that today a "school" is no longer a "schola," which means free time, but has become a highly complex industry that prepares people for an even more complex society, we might become receptive to the words of the Vietnamese Buddhist monk. If teaching means providing people with enough academic weapons to outdo other people, to make more money, to have a better career, and to get more esteem in the neighborhood, we had better start asking ourselves if there is any word from God that supports this approach.

The most universal and most appreciated role of the Christian ministry through the ages has been teaching. Wherever Christians went to be of service, they always considered teaching as one of their primary tasks because of their conviction that increasing insight into the human condition and the world is the way to new freedom and new ways of life. And although Christian churches frequently failed to live up to this conviction, even prevented the free growth of science and limited the fearless search for new fields of knowledge, Christians have always read in the Gospel a call to develop the human potentialities to the fullest through ongoing education.

The ministry of teaching has never limited itself, therefore, to the teaching of religion. Education is not primarily ministry because of what is taught but because of the nature of the educational process itself. Perhaps we have paid too much attention to the content of teaching without realizing that the teaching relationship is the most important factor in the ministry of teaching.

In this perspective, I raise the question: What do those who call themselves teachers or students really claim to be when they look at themselves in the light of the Gospel of Jesus Christ? In order to respond meaningfully to this question, I would like to describe two basic models of teaching—the violent model and the redemptive model—and then explicate our main resistances against learning.

By speaking in models, I will never do justice to individual teachers. I am not trying to. I only hope to map out basic structures that can help us to discover where we ourselves are and in which direction we want to go.

I. Teaching as a Violent Process

If we look at the overall educational situation today, it seems as if students are constantly confronted with the complicated problems of their world and almost daily presented with new skills, methods, and techniques to get these problems under control. In fields like medicine, sociology, psychology, chemistry, biology, economics, and even theology, there is an amazing preoccupation with manipulative devices and the degree to which they satisfy immediate needs, relate to urgent problems, and keep an acceptable balance in the style of our lives. "Getting things under control" is what keeps most teachers and students busy, and a successful teacher is often the individual who creates the conviction that humans have the necessary tools to tame the dangerous lion they will face as soon as they leave the training field.

As long as teaching takes place in this context, it is doomed to be a violent process and evoke a vicious cycle of action and reaction in which we face our world as new territory that has to be conquered but is filled with enemies unwilling to be ruled by a stranger. The teacher who enters this arena is forced to enter into a process which by its nature is competitive, unilateral, and alienating. In short: violent.

Let us have a closer look at these three characteristics of teaching as a violent process.

1. COMPETITIVE

Competition has become one of the most pervasive and also destructive aspects of modern education. The way some students look at other students and their teachers, the way they expect their grades and degrees, the way they prepare for their exams and take them, the way they apply to college and graduate school, and even the way in which they spend their free time; all this and much more is impregnated by an all-embracing sense of rivalry. You only have to walk on a college campus during the last week of a semester to pick up the mysterious "A, B, C, D, and F" language that seems to be on everyone's lips. The sadness of all this becomes clear when you see that a student is only happy with a high grade when other students have lower grades. It is obvious that in a system that encourages this ongoing competition, knowledge is no longer a gift that should be shared, but a property that should be defended.

Students who are aware of the fact that all their accomplishments, not only academic but athletic and social accomplishments as well, will be compared with those of others, and who realize that their grades will decide their further school-ing, their future job, and even their military status, under-standably can easily become victims of paralyzing fear.

This fear makes many students oversensitive to the reactions of their friends and teachers. This fear makes them extremely self-conscious, highly defensive in their relationships with others, constantly concerned about the possibility of failure, and very hesitant to take any risks or do anything unexpected. Often this fear becomes the unaccepted ruler over everything they write, say, or even think. Through this fear, competi-tion prevents students' free development as complete human persons.

To show how deeply this competition has permeated the educational system, I would like to take a closer look at one of the teaching methods, which at first glance seems to be the least competitive: the classroom discussion.

When you enter a college classroom today you will see that discussions have become an important part of modern educa-tion. The presupposition is that students learn more through discussion than through the absorption of ready-made infor-mation.

But is this always true? Quite often a closer analysis of an ongoing discussion shows that what in fact is happening is a sort of intellectual battle from which people tend to return more close-minded than when they entered it. Students sit-ting around the table, asking questions of their teacher or phrasing their ideas and opinions before each other, are often more like soldiers charging with rifles than friends shaking hands.

Quite often the process goes like this: A student enters into the discussion without knowing much about the subject to be discussed, but with both a desire to know more about it and a

fear of showing ignorance. As soon as someone states an opinion, the most common reaction is not the internal question:
"How can I understand *his* opinion better?" but "What is *my*
opinion?" So, too, does silence often mean more an occasion
to prepare an answer than to enter the train of thought of the
other. At once two, three, or more opinions are stated and the
primary concern becomes defense of the chosen position,
even when it is hardly worth defending. And so we see how
after a while people try to convince themselves and others of
ideas that in the beginning they hardly wanted to consider as
their own—ideas that were only meant as hesitant attempts to
participate in an exchange of thoughts. And how could it be
different when teachers are looked upon as those who are going to tell students, sooner or later, how much they are worth,
and when fellow students are rivals in the big fight for academic survival? Who wants to be weak and vulnerable in such
a situation? More importantly, who can really learn in this
way?

2. UNILATERAL

The second characteristic of the violent form of teaching is
that it is, in the final analysis, a unilateral process. Even the
many discussion methods, which suggest that people learn
from each other, can quite often be easily unmasked as simply
more acceptable ways to get a definitive message across or to
sell a so-called indispensable product. And when different
forms of discussion prove to be not much more than cheap
methods of advertisement, it is not so surprising that many
students become quickly irritated by them, complain that they
do not learn from them, and prefer straight lectures—which
at least dispense with reading another book.

This all goes to say that underneath many methods of

teaching is still the prevailing supposition that someone is competent and that someone else is not, and that the whole game is to try to make the one just as or nearly as competent as the other. When this ideal is realized, the teacher is no longer considered as a teacher and the student as a student, and both can depart with not much more accomplished than the ability to tell stories about each other as entertainment in their later years.

In this context the teacher is strong: the one who knows and should know. The student, however, is weak: the one who does not know and should want to know. The whole movement, therefore, is from teacher to student, from the strong to the weak, from one who knows to one who does not yet know. It is basically a unilateral process.

3. ALIENATING

Finally, the violent process of teaching is alienating, because the eyes of the student are directed outward, away from the self and toward relationships in the future where the "real" things are supposed to happen. School, then, comes to be seen as only a preparation for later life, for the "real" life. One day the classroom will at last be left behind, the books will be closed, the teacher forgotten, and life can begin. School is just an indoor training, a dry swim, a quasi-life. It is not surprising, therefore, that many students are bored and tired during class and are killing time by anxiously waiting until the bell rings and they can start doing their own thing. Nor is it so strange that many say they have nothing or little to do with what happens at school and must go by blind faith that one day they will be thankful for the knowledge they received.

It is not so strange then, that many teachers are looked upon as belonging to a world that is not the world of the students and that a hidden hostility often grows from this, expressing itself in a total lack of thankfulness toward those who have given much of their time, energy, and concern to prepare them for society.

This whole process is alienating because neither students nor teachers have been able to express their individuality or use their regular relationships with each other as a primary source of learning. They have been pulled away from their own experiences; they are staring out at the horizon, expecting something to appear there, while at the same time they have become blind to what is happening right in front of them.

When many people spend about twenty years in school, it can be asked how valuable their lives would have been if they were to die at the end of those twenty years. Do those twenty years serve only as a preparation for another twenty years which, in their turn, have to make possible a final twenty years of retirement? But when we do not really live here and now, why should we look forward to living somewhere else later? This is the core of alienation, a reality that is all too visible in the lives of many students and teachers.

We have now described the violent process of teaching as one that is competitive, unilateral, and alienating. While it might never be found in its total naked destructiveness, it should, nonetheless, be clear that elements of it can be detected in many of our contemporary educational methods.

Now we are ready to look at an alternative model, which I have called "redemptive." I would hope that the foregoing elaboration has created the desire to hear more about it.

II. Teaching as a Redemptive Process

If it is true that in many instances we have become the passive victims of an educational process whose impact on us we can hardly appreciate, it is imperative that we ask what exactly it is that has happened to us. As my first general impression, I suspect that too often we have lost contact with the source of our own existence and have become strangers in our own house. We tend to run around trying to solve the problems of our world while anxiously avoiding confrontation with that reality wherein our problems find their deepest roots: our own selves. In many ways we are like the busy executive who walks up to a precious flower and says: "What for God's sake are you doing here? Can't you get busy somehow?" and then finds the flower's response incomprehensible: "I am sorry, but I am just here to be beautiful."

How can we also come to this wisdom of the flower that being is more important than doing? How can we come to a creative contact with the grounding of our own life? Only through a teacher who can lead us to the source of our existence by showing us who we are and, thereby, what we are to do.

But where are these teachers? Some people think we have lost our real teachers and live in a time without wise guides. But is that really so? Or should we say that there are no teachers because there are no students? Teachers can only become teachers when there are students who allow them to be their teachers, and students can only become students when there are teachers who allow them to be their students. Only through this mutual acceptance can they enter into a teacher-student relationship that can be described as redemptive. In contrast to the violent form of teaching—which is competitive, unilateral, and alienating—therefore, the redemptive form of teaching can be described as evocative, bilateral, and actualizing. Let us examine these characteristics more closely.

1. EVOCATIVE

The first characteristic of a redemptive teacher-student relationship is that each tries to evoke in the other a certain potential, making them available to each other. A student who really wants to be taught must give the teacher freedom to become "teacher" by offering some personal life experiences as a source of insight and understanding. Only the student who allows access into his or her own personal life experience can evoke in another the possibility of becoming a real teacher. In this sense, teachers depend completely on their students to give them trust, confidence, and friendship, and to share with their teachers their weaknesses, strengths, desires, and needs. Do not conclude too quickly that this is unrealistic. There are, in fact, classrooms in which discussions become evocative forms of learning, where students are able to offer their own experiences to their teachers and fellow students in order to facilitate a deeper understanding. In such cases, instead of the famous "Yes, but . . ." dialogue, you will hear, "tell me more," or "that reminds me of . . ." or "I could add something to that." Competition is absent, and the teacher is no longer the fear-inspiring judge but rather the one given the opportunity to be teacher and the one who invites the students to become more and more accessible to learning. Perhaps teachers can never be true teachers unless they are, to a certain degree, friends. In other words, when Christ said to His disciples: "I shall not call you servants anymore, but friends," (John 15:14), he became in truth their real teacher because now the relationship was without fear, and real learning could begin.

2. BILATERAL

The second characteristic of a redemptive teaching relationship is that it is bilateral. This means that not only does the student have to learn from the teacher but, conversely, the teacher has to learn from the student. When a teacher is unwilling to become a student and recognize the students as teachers, there is no redemptive process. Teachers and students must together search for what is true, meaningful, and valid, and give each other the chance to play each other's role.

Few teachers, however, feel free enough to allow their students to know more than they, let alone to leave their students free enough to learn from them. They tend to think that they lose respect and esteem when they allow their students to guide them and, in so doing, they fail to realize that it is exactly this freedom that will create the relationship by which they will be able to redeem the students from fear and give the students freedom to grow. In this process, moreover, it is not so much the intellectual superiority of the teacher that counts as it is maturity to face the unknown and willingness to leave unanswerable questions unanswered.

If the teaching process is bilateral, it is essentially open-ended. Discussion is no longer a method to get a well-prepared opinion across to the student, but an exchange of experiences and ideas whose outcome is not determined. In this way, discussion might well lead to new and surprising perspectives and insights.

When teacher and students are willing to be influenced by each other, learning can become a creative process that can hardly be boring or tiring. It is only through a relationship of this sort that learning takes place.

3. ACTUALIZING

This brings us to the third aspect of teaching as a redemptive process: It is not alienating but actualizing. This is to say that if learning is to be in some way a preparation for the future, it can only be so when the future becomes a part of the teaching relationship here and now. To build a better world, the beginnings of that world must be visible in daily life. There is no reason to expect much to happen in the future if the signs of hope are not made visible in the present. We cannot speak about ways to bring about peace and freedom if we cannot draw from our own experiences of peace and freedom here and now. We cannot commit ourselves to work for justice and love in tomorrow's society if we cannot discover the seeds of it in the relationships we engage in today. A nonviolent world cannot be born out of a violent teaching process any more than justice can be born out of jealousy, mildness out of cruelty, or love out of hate. But when schools are places where community can be experienced, where people can live together without fear of each other, and where learning can be based on a creative exchange of experiences and ideas, then there is a chance that those who come from them will have an increasing desire to bring about in the world what they experienced during their years of formation. In this sense, schools are not training camps to prepare people to enter into a violent society, but places where redemptive forms of society can be experimented with and offered to the modern world as alternative styles of life. Teaching can then become a way of creating a new lifestyle in which people are able to relate to each other in a basically nonviolent way. And in trying to live this way, the teacher also discovers that learning is a "way of life" that goes far beyond the classroom situation. This type of learning creates new relationships that do not end when students leave but that ask for continuation, not limited by grades and degrees; a challenge to an ongoing renewal of one's style of life.

We have now described the redemptive process of teaching as an evocative, bilateral, and actualizing process. This ideal obviously will never be fully realized. But if we are able to realize at least the beginnings of it in our own situation, we might be encouraged to take the reins of the horse into our hands and lead it away from violence and toward increasing freedom. Nonetheless, we would indeed be fooling ourselves if we thought the choice of a redemptive form of teaching was obvious. If this were the case, all of what I have written thus far would be superfluous. The choice, however, is not obvious because we are faced with a deep-seated human resistance against learning. It is toward this resistance that we must now turn in order to better understand it and thereby be able to remove it.

III. Resistance Against Learning

Learning is meant to lead to a redemptive insight into the condition of our world. But do we always desire insight? The Jesuit theologian Bernard Lonergan writes:

> Just as insight can be desired, so too, it can be unwanted. Beside the love of light, there can be a love of darkness. If prepossessions and prejudices notoriously vitiate theoretical investigations, much more easily can elementary passions bias understanding in practical and personal matters. To exclude an insight is also to exclude the further questions that would arise from it and the complementary insights that would carry it towards a rounded and balanced viewpoint.

To lack that fuller view results in behavior that generates misunderstanding both in ourselves and in others. To suffer such incomprehension favours a withdrawal from the outer drama of human living into the inner drama of phantasy. (From *Insight*, Longmans Green and Co., Ltd., London, 1957, p. 191.)

Lonergan calls such an aberration of understanding a "scotosis," derived from the Greek word *skotos*, which means "darkness," and the resultant blind spot a "scotoma." By introducing these terms, he has helped us to come to a better understanding of the massive resistance against learning, for it is exactly this scotosis that prevents us from really dealing with those factors that are crucial to our growth. By this scotosis, this exclusion of painful insights, we prevent our own experience from becoming part of the learning process and become like unengaged spectators in the procession of life.

I am trying to say very simple and obvious things here. But if it is true that the most obvious things can easily become the most threatening things to us, then perhaps they also can become the easiest subjects of scotosis.

Scotosis means long and fierce discussions about justice and equality while we hate our teacher or ignore the needs of others around us. Scotosis means endless academic quarrels in a world filled with atrocities, and much talk about hunger from people suffering from overweight. Scotosis allows church people to indulge in comfortable discussions about the Kingdom of God while they should know that God is with the poor, the sick, the hungry, and the dying. In Lonergan's words, "Scotosis means an aberration which prevents the emergence into consciousness of perspectives that would give rise to unwanted insights" (op. cit., p. 192). It is indeed startling to discover how we keep ourselves free from those unwanted insights.

Why is this scotosis so difficult to heal? What keeps us blind to the obvious? If we could find some answers to these questions, we could begin, at least in part, to understand why there is such a powerful resistance to learning and why it is so difficult for teaching to become a redemptive process.

I would like to suggest three factors that keep us from learning and at the same time might explain many of our teacher-student scotomas: (1) a wrong supposition, (2) a false pressure, and (3) a horror of self-encounter.

1. A WRONG SUPPOSITION

Many teachers, as well as many students, still operate under the faulty supposition that it is better to give than to receive. Teachers want to give something to students—an idea, an opinion, a specific skill, advice, or any other thing they think students are waiting for—and students, in turn, value their teachers according to what they have to give.

It is difficult to recognize the meaning of Christ's saying, "There is more happiness in giving than in receiving" (Acts 20:35), because it is difficult to confess that perhaps the greatest service we can offer to each other is to receive and allow the other the happiness of giving. Much of the happiness in our lives is derived from the fact that we can give and that our friends have been willing to receive our gifts, to make them a part of our lives, and to allow themselves to become dependent on us through them. We feel happy when we see the pictures we gave our friends displayed most advantageously on walls of their homes. The question is: Would we have given them the freedom to put them in the attic?

A gift only becomes a gift when it is received; and noth-

ing we have to give—wealth, talents, competence, or just
beauty—will ever be recognized as true gifts until someone is
open to accept them.

This all suggests that those who want others to grow—that
is, to discover their potential and capacities, to experience that
they have something to live and work for—should first of all
be able to recognize their own gifts and be willing to receive
them. For we become fully human only when we are received
and accepted. In this way, many students could be better students if there were someone who affirmed their capacities and
accepted them as real gifts. Students grow during those moments in which they discover that they have offered something
new to their teachers without making them feel threatened
but, rather, thankful. And teachers could be much better
teachers if students were willing to draw the best out of them
and show their acceptance by thankfulness and creative work.
Too many people cling to their own talents and leave them un-
touched because they are afraid that nobody is really interested.
They then regress into their own fantasies and suffer from a
growing loss of self-esteem.

As long as we keep living with the wrong supposition that
giving is our first task, our scotosis cannot be healed, and the
most creative insights will stay out of our consciousness.

2. A FALSE PRESSURE

A second reason that prevents our scotosis from healing is
that we are caught in the deadly network of a modern educational process that makes us believe we are better and more
competent when we have better grades, higher degrees, and
more academic rewards. A great many hours are spent by both
teachers and students in trying to keep up with the physically
and mentally exhausting routine of academic life. We have put

such a high value on degrees and certificates that we are willing to entrust ourselves blindly to someone with an M.A. or a Ph.D. who, only a few months ago, was struggling with exams and would have qualified as one of those irresponsible, rebellious students.

This false pressure of society, which forces us to pay undue attention to the formal recognition of our intellectual accomplishments, tends to pull us away from our own more personal needs and to prevent us from achieving insights into our own experiences that can form the basis of a creative life project.

3. A HORROR OF SELF-ENCOUNTER

The final and most powerful resistance against learning, however, is much more profound. It is the resistance against a conversion that calls for a "kenotic" self-encounter. We can be creatively receptive and break out of the imprisoning chains of academic conformity only when we can squarely face our fundamental human condition and fully experience it as the foundation of all learning in which both students and teachers are involved. It is the experience that teacher and student are both sharing the same reality—that is, they are both naked, powerless, destined to die, and, in the final analysis, totally alone and unable to save each other or anyone else. It is the embarrassing discovery of solidarity in weakness and of a desperate need to be liberated from slavery. It is the confession that they both live in a world filled with unrealities and that they allow themselves to be driven by the most trivial desires and the most distasteful ambitions.

Only if students and teachers are willing to face this painful reality can they free themselves for real learning. For only in the depths of loneliness, when they have nothing to lose and are no longer clinging to life as to an inalienable property, can they become sensitive to what is really happening in the world and be able to approach it without fear.

This conversion, which is not a sudden event but an ongoing process, is the most important prerequisite for arriving at redemptive insights and removing our many blind spots.

So we have seen how a wrong supposition, false pressure, and horror of self-encounter make it extremely difficult to heal our scotosis, to take away our resistance against learning, and to make a redemptive form of teaching a real possibility.

Conclusion

The core idea of this chapter has been that ultimately we can only come from a violent form of teaching to a redemptive form of teaching through a conversion that pervades our total personality and breaks the power of our resistance against learning.

Jesus can be called Teacher in the fullest sense of the word precisely because He did not cling to His prerogatives but became one of the many who have to learn. His life makes it clear to us that we do not need weapons, that we do not need to hide ourselves or play competitive games with each other. Only when we are not afraid to show our weakness, and when we allow ourselves to be touched by the tender hand of the Teacher, will we become real students. For if education is meant to challenge the world, it is Christ Himself who challenges teachers as well as students to give up their defenses and to become available for real growth. In order to

come to this conversion, which is the healing of our scotomas, we might be thrown from our horses and be blind for
a while, but in the end we will be brought to an entirely new
insight, which might well bring about a new person in a new
world.

❧

CHAPTER II

Beyond the Retelling of the Story

Preaching

Insight and Availability

Introduction

In 1857, Anthony Trollope wrote in *Barchester Towers*: "There is, perhaps, no greater hardship at present inflicted on mankind in civilised and free countries, than the necessity of listening to sermons" (cf., *U.S. Catholic*, July 1970, "Let's Abolish the Sunday Sermon," by Daphne D. C. Pochin Mould). I would not be surprised to find many people today who are willing to agree with him.

The more amazing it is, therefore, that there are still so many preachers who want to preach and so many people who are willing to listen. Why is this so? Perhaps because people today, just as they did a century ago, have a lasting desire to come to an insight into their own condition, and the condition of their world, such that they can be free to follow Christ: that is, to live their lives just as authentically as He lived His. The purpose of preaching is none other than to help them to come to this basic insight.

Insight is more than intellectual understanding; it is knowledge through and through, knowledge to which whole persons can say Yes. It is an understanding that pervades us from head to heart, from top to toe, from brain to guts. When we can come to this totally permeating knowledge, we will be able to really listen to the Word of God and to follow the light that entered into our darkness. In this way, one of the most crucial purposes of preaching is to remove these real and all-too-visible obstacles that cause us to listen without understanding.

Not too long ago, during Sunday Mass in a Dutch church, a friend of mine gave a sermon on which he had spent at least three days of preparation. After the service, I saw a seventeen-year-old girl sitting in the last pew. Since I had helped my friend with his sermon, I was curious to find out how people felt about it. I walked over to the girl and said: "Say, how did you like that sermon?" She looked at me as if I could not have asked a sillier question, brushed her hair away from her eyes, and said: "Sir, I never listen to sermons. That's the time when I take my nap." Thrown somewhat off-balance by her response, I looked around to find someone who could give me a little more support. When I saw a man in his thirties, walking out of the church with his wife and children, I stopped him, saying: "Excuse me, Sir—can I ask you a question? What did you think about the sermon to-day?" He immediately responded: "Well, that priest certainly looked like a nice young man—but I think he still has a lot to learn. All that talk about Camillo Torres and Martin Luther King—and that we all should help to change the church—you know, Sir? I wish they would let *me* get up on that pulpit and say something. Sometimes my hands are just itching and I'm about to stand up and say something back—but my wife feels that I say enough at home and should at least be quiet in church."

The girl's indifference and the man's irritation are two re-actions to preaching that prevent many people from listening to those ministers and priests who are trying their best to reach the hundreds of people still willing to visit their churches on Sunday. If insight is the purpose of preaching, and if indifference and irritation are two of the main obstacles that confront it, we find ourselves right in the middle of the problem of preaching.

Preaching belongs to the heart of the Christian ministry. Historians, systematic theologians, and especially biblical scholars all have many contributions to offer for a better understanding of this crucial ministerial task. It would, however, be extremely presumptuous to even try to touch upon the many aspects of preaching. Therefore, I would like to limit myself to just one question: "What kind of person is it who can help take away those obstacles that prevent the Word of God from falling on fertile ground?"

The question is really about the spirituality of the preacher. But before we can realistically approach it, we must first take a close look at two of the main difficulties in preaching: One is in the message itself, and the other is in the messenger. Therefore, I would like to divide this chapter into three parts: (1) the problem of the message, (2) the problem of the messenger, and (3) the one who gives insight.

I. The Problem of the Message

In order to bring any kind of message to people, there has to be at least the willingness to accept the message. This willingness means some desire to listen, some question that asks for an answer, or some general feeling of uncertainty that needs clarification or understanding. But whenever an answer is given when there is no question, or when support is offered when there is no need, or when an idea is given when there

is no desire to know, the only possible effect can be irritation
or indifference.

It is no secret that those who address themselves to people
in church find quite often that a high percentage of the people present have little eagerness to listen. And when teachers
and lecturers express a certain jealousy in regard to the many
people who come under the influence of a preacher, they tend
to forget that there are few audiences so little motivated to listen as a church congregation. What causes this lack of motivation? I suspect there are two aspects of the message that can
explain at least part of this phenomenon: the redundancy of
the message, and the fearfulness of the message.

1. THE REDUNDANCY OF THE MESSAGE

If we say that preaching means announcing the good news,
it is important to realize that for most people there is absolutely no news in the sermon. Practically nobody listens to
a sermon with the expectation of hearing something they do
not already know. They have heard about Jesus—His disciples, His savings miracles, His death and resurrection—at
home, in kindergarten, in grade school, in high school, and in
college so often and in so many different ways and forms that
the last thing they expect to come from a pulpit is any news.
And the core of the Gospel—"You must love the Lord your
God with all your heart, with all your soul, and with all your
mind and you must love your neighbor as yourself"—has
been repeated so often and so persistently that it has lost, for
the majority of people, even the slightest possibility of evok-
ing any response. They have heard it from the time of their
earliest childhood and will continue to hear it until they are
dead—unless, of course, they become so bored on the way
that they refuse to place themselves any longer in a situation

in which they will be exposed to this redundant information. It is fascinating to see how people sit up straight, eyes wide open, when the preacher starts the sermon with a little secular story by way of appetizer, but immediately turn on their sleeping signs and curl up in a more comfortable position when the famous line comes: "And this, my brothers and sisters, is exactly what Jesus meant when He said . . ." From then on, most preachers are alone, relying only of the volume of their voices or the idiosyncrasies of their movements to keep in contact. It is indeed sad to say that the name of Jesus has lost most of its mobilizing power for many people. Too often the situation is like the one in the Catholic school where the teacher asked: "Children, who invented the steam engine?" Everyone was silent until finally a little boy sitting in the back of the class raised his finger and said in a dull voice and with watery eyes: "I guess it's Jesus again."

When a message has become so redundant that it has completely lost the ability to evoke any kind of creative response, it can hardly be considered a message any longer. And if you feel you cannot avoid hearing the message physically at its presentation, you can at least close your eyes and mind and drop out.

2. THE FEARFULNESS OF THE MESSAGE

But redundancy is only one aspect of the message that prevents people from listening. And even though it may be realistic to admit that there is hardly any news in the sermon for most people, the core message of the Gospel nonetheless contains a Truth that no one has yet fully made true. And real listening means nothing less than the constant willingness to confess that you have not yet realized what you profess to believe. Who likes to hear, for example, that the last will be first, if he happens to be first? And who wants to hear that those who are poor, who mourn, who are hungry, thirsty, and persecuted are called happy, when she is wealthy, self-content, well-fed, praised for her good wines, and admired by all her friends? Who wants to hear that he has to love his enemies and pray for those who persecute him when he thinks his boss is an S.O.B., calls his own son a good-for-nothing bum, and glows with pride when he reads that the troops in Iraq have captured another city? The message might be the same all through life and might be repeated over and over again in different words and styles, but those who will let it really come through allow themselves, at the same time, the possibility of coming to an insight that might well have consequences for their style of life, which they are not eager to accept. The truth, after all, is radical: It goes to the roots of life in such a way that few are those who want it and the freedom it brings with it. There is, in fact, such an outright fear of facing the Truth in all its directness and simplicity that irritation and anger seem to be more common human responses than a humble confession that one also belongs to the group Jesus criticized. In this way, many breakfast discussions on Sunday, for example, are nothing less than clear-cut attempts to undo any possible effects of the threatening Truth. When someone says, "I wish I could get up there and tell those preachers how life is when you're married and have three kids," that person is often expressing what is in fact a deep-seated resistance to confess that the Gospel is also speaking to families. And just as indifference can make us unavailable to the word of the Gospel, so too can irritation bar the way for new and liberating insights.

Redundancy of the message and fear of the Truth seem to be the two basic reasons why preachers have such difficulty coming close to their people. This is perhaps even more the case when those who are present scarcely feel free to walk out. Many still feel bound to some distant authority in Heaven, Rome, Canterbury, or the chancellery who has convinced them that if they are unwilling to suffer one hour a week, they will surely suffer a great deal more when all their weeks have passed. As a result, a preacher is again facing an extremely hard task: to proclaim the good news, which for many is neither new nor good.

Before we can ask what kind of person will be able to break through this deep-seated human resistance against the message, we have to be honest enough to confess that it is not just the message but also the messenger who often keeps people away from painful but liberating insights.

II. The Problem of the Messenger

Many preachers tend to increase the resistance against listening, instead of decreasing it, with the way in which they tend to get their eternal message across. A critical analysis of many sermons would show that the Prophet Isaiah was correct when he said: "You will listen and not understand, see—and not perceive" (Isaiah 6:9–10). It would prove useful, then, to have a closer look at a few ways of preaching that might make us better understand the problem of the messenger. In this regard, I would suggest that the two main reasons why a preacher often creates more antagonism than sympathy are (1) the assumption of nonexistent feelings and (2) preoccupation with a theological point of view.

1. NONEXISTENT FEELINGS

A large number of sermons start by making untested suppositions. Without hesitation, many preachers impose feelings, ideas, questions, and problems on their listeners that are often completely unknown to the majority of them, if not to all. Some preachers make their congregations ask themselves why their chasubles are red on Pentecost, why the last Sunday of the liturgical year is not in December, why Lent lasts forty days, why All Souls' Day is immediately after All Saints' Day—questions that people could not care less about and which are usually left-over problems from the minister's own vague memories of volumes of pious literature.

Sometimes whole sermons are built on clerical feelings that are quite alien to lay people. I remember one sermon that began as follows:

> Today we all congregate together to celebrate the ascension of our Lord Jesus Christ. Only a few weeks ago our hearts were filled with joy because of the resurrection of our Lord, and now already we feel with the Apostles the sadness about His leaving us. But let us not despair, because Jesus does not leave us alone but is going to send us the Holy Spirit within a few days. And not only for the Apostles but also for this community gathered around His altar the Spirit will bring new life and new hope . . .

It came as no surprise to find that everyone was mentally absent by the time the preacher finished the introduction. I counted about thirty people scattered in the big, mostly empty church. Nobody seemed to remember how happy they were at Easter or to realize how sad they had been on Ascension Day. There was no congregation, no celebration, no community, certainly no despair or desire to have the Holy Spirit come soon. There were only a couple of isolated individuals who had kept in mind that Ascension Day is a day of obligation and were faithful enough to go to Mass.

Even more irritating than this, however, are preachers who somehow seem to know exactly how everybody feels. A good example is the following introduction:

> Brothers and Sisters in Christ,
> In a time in which we all have become part of the rat race, in which we are forced to become victims of our watches and slaves of our agenda, in which we are running from one committee meeting to another, we have become deaf to the voice of God who speaks in silence and in the quiet moments of prayer.

Well, this certainly tells us a lot about the preacher—but what about the grandmother who spent a good part of the week solving crossword puzzles, what about the boy who just came back from the baseball field, and his teacher who spent Saturday reading Dostoyevsky, and what about the housewife who enjoyed a nice afternoon with her young child at the city zoo?

Perhaps someone in the audience might say Yes to the preacher, but most will feel just as far from those words as they feel from the so-called rat race. They might not be aware of this, but in one way or another—by a protective numbness or an outright expression of hostility—they will show that they are not really present.

2. THEOLOGICAL PREOCCUPATION

A second and even more difficult problem to overcome is the theological preoccupation of the preacher. Some preachers become so excited about a book they have recently read or a new viewpoint they have heard that they feel compelled to have others share their enthusiasm. They quickly and, as it often happens, disappointingly find out, however, that Karl

Rahner, Harvey Cox, or Schillebeeckx do not appeal as much, if at all, to their hearers as to themselves. The main reason is not that their theological ideas are not valid or meaningful, but rather that not only those who preach but also those who listen have their own "theologies." Let me explain this with a story.

A theology student was asked to give a sermon about the Kingdom of God. She carefully studied the Scriptures and read the latest literature on the subject. But when she thought she had a clear idea about the Kingdom of God and was ready to present her sermon, the suggestion was made to her to first visit four families living in the parish where she was going to preach and ask them what they thought about the Kingdom of God.

So she went first to a meteorologist, a scholarly man who had read many books in his life and had discovered that making predictions was a pretty tricky business. And the meteorologist said: "The Kingdom of God is the fulfillment of God's promises, and God's people have to refrain from the unhealthy curiosity of exactly how this will happen."

Then the student went to a storekeeper, whose business had been a failure and whose wife had been sick for many years. And the storekeeper said: "The Kingdom of God is Heaven—where I finally will receive my reward for enduring my hard, bothersome life."

From the storekeeper she went to a wealthy farmer, who had a strong wife and two beautiful and healthy children. And the farmer said: "The Kingdom of God is a beautiful garden where we will all continue the happy life we started in this world."

Finally, the student came to the house of a laborer, who had learned a good trade and was proud that he was able to earn his money with his own hands. And the laborer said: "The

Kingdom of God was a smart invention of the Church to keep
the illiterate happy and the poor content, but since I can take
care of myself and have a good job I have no need any more
for a kingdom to come."

When the theology student came home from these visits
and read her sermon again, she realized suddenly that her ideas
were close to those of the meteorologist, who was used to living with uncertainties, but that the storekeeper looking for a
reward, the farmer hoping for the continuation of his happiness, and the laborer who saw the Kingdom in the works of
his own hands would not understand her. And when she read
the Scriptures again she discovered that there was a place for
all four of her parishioners in the Kingdom of God. (These
data are used with the permission of Mr. Leo Lans, student of
Catholic Theological Institute in Utrecht, Holland.)

Perhaps the greatest temptation of preachers is to think that
only they have a theology and to believe that the best thing to
do is to convert all those who listen to their way of thinking.
In this way, however, they have failed to realize that in a very
real sense they haven't loved their neighbors as themselves,
since they have not taken the neighbors' views and experiences as seriously as their own. When this is true, in fact, many
of those who listen to their viewpoint will become indifferent
or irritated without exactly knowing why. And preachers who
spend a great deal of time studying books and preparing sermons will become more and more disillusioned as they start
to feel that nobody wants to listen to the Word of God. All
the while, however, they have forgotten that God's Word does
not have to be exactly the same as their own. When preachers address nonexistent feelings and are anxiously preoccupied
with their own theology, they tend to increase, instead of decrease, the already-existing resistance against the message.

At this point, one might well be inclined to ask how

preachers can overcome this problem. From the outset, however, we have to say that the question itself is misdirected, for there is no tool, no technique, no special skill that can solve the problem. But perhaps there is a "spirituality"—a way of living—that can give hope to those who want to bring their people to a liberating insight that can make them free to follow Christ. Let us, therefore, now examine the kind of person who can help others to come to this insight.

III. The One Who Gives Insight

The task of preaching is to assist in the ongoing struggle of becoming. And this is accomplished primarily by speaking about Jesus Christ, Who lived His life with an increasing willingness to face His own condition and the condition of the world in which He found Himself, in such a way that encourages us to follow Him; that is, to live our lives with the same authenticity even if it leads us to tears, sweat, and possibly a violent death.

All preachers are called to endeavor to take away the obstacles that prevent this painful process of becoming human. This is a difficult task, since there seems to be in us a profound resistance to change, at least when it concerns our basic outlook on life. Once we have a more or less satisfying standpoint, we tend to cling to it, since it always seems better to have at least a poor standpoint than to have none at all. In this sense we are often quite conservative. We seem to be constantly tempted to deny our most precious human ability—which is to shift standpoints—and we often settle for the comfortable routine. In many ways our human nature is resistant to the call of Him Who says that when you are young you can put on your own belt and walk where you like, but when you grow old you will stretch your hands and some-body else will put a belt round you and take you where you would rather not go (John 21:18). In complete contrast to our idea that adulthood means the ability to take care of oneself, Jesus describes it as a growing willingness to stretch out one's hands and be guided by others.

It is no wonder, then, that ministers who hope to remove the obstacles of this process of growth and to have people be-come free to surrender themselves and let others gird them are considered men and women of courage.

The two aspects of preaching that seem to be most essen-tial for a preacher to facilitate this ongoing process of becom-ing are (1) dialogue and (2) availability.

1. THE CAPACITY FOR DIALOGUE

When I use the word "dialogue," I do not think about di-alogue homilies in which everyone shares, nor about a public discussion, or any other specific technique to make people participate. No, nothing of that is meant by the word "dia-logue"; I simply mean a way of relating to men and women so that they are able to respond to what is said with their own life experience. In this way, dialogue is not a technique but an attitude of the preacher who is willing to enter into a rela-tionship in which partners can really influence each other. In a true dialogue, the one announcing the Word cannot stay on the outside. Those who preach cannot remain untouchable and invulnerable. Rather, they need to be totally and most personally involved. This can be a completely internal process in which there is no verbal exchange of words, but it requires the risk of real engagement in the relationship between those who speak and those who listen. Only then can we have a real dialogue.

When this dialogue takes place, those who listen will come to the recognition of who they really are, since the words of the preacher will find a sounding board in their own hearts and find anchoring places in their personal life-experiences. And when they allow the words to come so close as to become their flesh and blood, they can say: "What you say loudly, I whispered in the dark; what you pronounce so clearly, I had some suspicion about; what you put in the foreground, I felt in the back of my mind; what you hold so firmly in your hand always slipped away through my fingers. Yes, I find myself in your words because your words come from the depths of human experiences and, therefore, are not just yours but also mine, and your insights do not just belong to you, but are mine as well."

When this happens, there is a real dialogue. When this happens, the barriers fall down and our hearts are opened to accept the goodness of the news! When this happens, we are able as human beings to recognize real dialogue and affirmation that allow us to accept our deficiencies and mistakes and our desperate need for the Word of God that has the power to set us free. But when we are not connected with what is going on within, when we do not know what we really want, feel, or do, then words that come from above cannot penetrate into our center. When emotions, ideas, and aspirations are tangled together under an impermeable crust of fear and unknowing, no dew can bring forth fruits and no clouds can "rain the just."

But whenever, anxious and seemingly impenetrable, we are approached by one who expresses solidarity with us, offering insight and understanding as sources of recognition and clarification, then our confusion disperses and paths are opened that can lead us farther into the light. Then the meteorologist, the storekeeper, the farmer, and the laborer may realize that the one announcing the Word is simply taking away the veil that prevented them from seeing their own very experience. That is when they and we recognize that the Word of God is not a boring repetition of one person's reflection but a dynamic call for us to grow.

A beautiful example of this dialogue is the sermon given by William Sloane Coffin, Jr., in Battell Chapel in New Haven, Connecticut, on April 10, 1970, during the days of the Panther trial. He started this sermon with the following words:

> Most of us who are here today are in deep distress. The Panther trial is polarizing not only our Yale-New Haven community and increasingly the entire nation; it is also polarizing ourselves. The innermost feelings of many of us are now so sharply divided that they are destroying our capacity to think and act with anything approaching conviction and compassion. (*Yale Daily News*, Monday, April 20, 1970.)

That is the dialogue, and because many in Coffin's audience could say "Yes, we recognize our paralysis," this recognition inspired in them their desire to move again and do something. The words of Coffin that followed were so effective because his listeners were ready for them. It is no surprise that this sermon was an important contribution to the creative response to the fearful situation in New Haven.

But again, dialogue is not a technique or a special skill that you can learn in school, but a way of life. Nobody can imitate Coffin or any other effective preacher. In the final analysis, dialogue can only become actual through a willingness on the part of the preacher to be available to the people in a very ba-

sic sense. And so, I would finally like to examine this availability as the spiritual core for ministers of the Word of God.

2. AVAILABILITY

Availability is the primary condition for every dialogue that
leads to inspiration and redemptive insight. Ministers who are
not willing to allow their own understanding of faith, their
own doubts, anxieties, hopes, fears, and joys, to be available as
a source of recognition for others can never expect to remove
the many obstacles that prevent the Word of God from bear-
ing fruit.

So it is here that we touch precisely upon the spirituality of
the ministers of God's Word. In order to be available to others, we, as ministers, must be available to ourselves first of all.
And we know how extremely difficult it is to be available to
ourselves, to have our own experiences at our disposal. We
know how selective our self-understanding really is. If we are
optimists, we are apt to remember those events of the day that
tend to reinforce our positive outlook on life. If we are pes-
simists, we might say to ourselves, "Again, another day that
proves that I am no good."

But we must try to become more realistic, allowing all our
experiences to be ours, and accepting our happiness as well as
our sadness, our hate as well as our love, all as really belonging to our own human experience. When ministers do not
have all their experiences at their disposal, they tend to make
available to others only those that fit best the image they want
to have of themselves before their listeners. And this is exactly
what we call "closed-mindedness." It is blindness. It is closing
off an essential part of our precious human reality.

Those who want to be real leaders are those who are able
to put the full range of their life-experiences—their experi-

ences in prayer, in conversation, and in their lonely hours—at the disposal of those who ask them to announce the Word of God. Pastoral care does not mean running around nervously trying to redeem people, to save them at the last moment, or to put them on the right track by a good idea, an intelligent remark, or practical advice. No! We are already redeemed once and for all. Pastoral care means, in the final analysis: offering your own life-experiences to your brothers and sisters and, as Paul Simon sings, to lay yourself down like a bridge over troubled water.

I am not saying that you should talk about yourself, your personal worries, your family, your youth, your illnesses, or your hang-ups. Doing that has nothing to do with availability. That is only playing a narcissistic game with your own idiosyncrasies. No, I mean we who speak God's Word are called to experience life to such a depth that the meteorologist, the storekeeper, the farmer, and the laborer will all one day or another realize that we are actually experiencing life in places where their own lives also really vibrate, and in this way we allow them to become free to let the Word of God do its redemptive work. Because, as Carl Rogers says: "What is most personal is most general" (*On Becoming a Person*, Houghton Mifflin, New York, 1961, p. 26). Thomas Oden explains this when he writes:

> Repeatedly I have found, to my astonishment, that the feelings which have seemed to me most private, most personal, and therefore the feelings I least expect to be understood by others, when clearly expressed, resonate deeply and consistently with others' own experiences. This has led me to believe that what I experience in the most unique and personal way, if brought to clear expression, is precisely

what others are most deeply experiencing in analogous ways. (*The Structure of Awareness*, Abingdon Press, Nashville and New York, 1969, pp. 23–24.)

When people listen to one who is really inwardly available to personal life-experience and, therefore, able to offer this experience as a source of recognition, they no longer have to be afraid to face their own condition or that of their world, because the one who stands in front of them is the living witness that insight liberates and does not create new anxieties. Only then can indifference and irritation be removed; only then can the Word of God, which has been repeated so often but understood so little, find fertile ground and take root in their hearts and minds.

So we have seen how, through availability, a real dialogue can take place that can lead to new insight. This is to say that the Word of God, which is a sign of contradiction and a sword piercing the heart of all people, can only reach us when it has become the flesh and blood of the one who announces it.

Conclusion

I have used a lot of words to say a very simple thing: Ministers are people who are willing to give their lives for their people. The Word of God is always coming into the world, though it is often met with indifference and irritation. Those who preach are called upon to remove these obstacles and lead folks to the true insights that eventually set them free.

If we who are privileged to announce God's word do not want to increase the resistance against the Good News, but to decrease it, we have to be willing to lay ourselves down and make our own suffering and our own hope available to others, so that they too can find their own, often difficult way. Nobody can ever claim to be a real preacher in this sense. Only Christ could, since only He entered into a full dialogue with those He loved by laying down His life in total availability. But out of all those who witnessed His death and saw the blood and water come from His pierced side, only a few were willing to cast off their indifference and irritation and come to the liberating insight: "In truth this was the son of God" (Matthew 27:54).

Every time real preaching occurs, the crucifixion is realized again: For no minister of God's Word can bring anyone to the light without having personally entered into the darkness of the Cross. Perhaps Anthony Trollope was right when he said that the necessity of listening to sermons is the greatest hardship inflicted on people in civilized and free countries. But if we want our countries to become really free and civilized, let us hope that there will always be those who are willing to endure the hardship of preaching and thus leading people through darkness to the Light of God.

➤

CHAPTER III

Beyond the Skillful Response

Individual Pastoral Care

Competence and Contemplation

Introduction

In order to deal concretely and specifically with the relationship between individual pastoral care and the spirituality of the minister, I would like to start this chapter with the story of Michael Smith, a pastoral trainee at Stone Memorial Hospital. The head of the section where Michael was working told him that one of the patients, a Mrs. Kern, had cancer and was in very critical condition, and that a visit might be worthwhile.

Michael, dressed in a white coat like the medical interns but with a name tag identifying him as a chaplain, entered Mrs. Kern's room for a pastoral visit. There the following conversation took place:

MRS. KERN: You're a new one. I don't believe I've seen you among the doctors.

MICHAEL: You haven't, I'm sure, though I was meaning to call on you sooner. I should have been here sooner than this. I'm one of the chaplains, Chaplain Smith.

MRS. KERN: How do you do?

MICHAEL: I just want to say hello to you. I want to let you

know that we're around, and that we'll be happy to help in any way we can. The chaplain's office answers on extension 2765, and in case you're interested, there are services here on Sunday—several ecumenical and one Mass for Catholics.

MRS. KERN: I am Jewish.

MICHAEL: Oh, fine. You may be interested to know that though he is not here daily, a rabbi makes regular visits here at Stone Memorial. Could I call him for you?

MRS. KERN: Please do not. I would prefer not to bother him— or anyone.

MICHAEL: If you wish. How ill have you been?

MRS. KERN: Enough to die, but I don't! And all this doctoring has been done and does no good—it's a continual torture. But I do not care to talk. Will you please excuse me?

MICHAEL: I'm sure that I've come in at a very inopportune time, and I hope that I haven't disturbed or upset you. Still, I would like to drop in from time to time, if for no other reason than to say hello, just to see how things are with you.

MRS. KERN: You would indeed be doing me a very great favor—and would be respecting my wishes perfectly, as I have told the doctors—if you and everyone else would leave me entirely alone. My own family, except for my husband, do not come to see me. I have told my daughter not to come. I don't want her to see me in this condition. Yet people insist. Even a dying animal—*a dying animal*—can crawl off by itself to die. I repeat: You will be doing me a favor if you leave—and do not return.

Back at his room, Michael wrote: "I feel discouraged, even guilty. It was almost as if I had been kicked in the stomach."

(This case is used with the permission of Dr. Seward Hiltner of Princeton Theological Seminary.)

This painful visit and the even more painful reflection on it raises three questions that have been raised over and over again in respect to individual pastoral care.

1. Who are you, Michael, to visit Mrs. Kern?
2. What kind of relationship do you expect to have with this patient?
3. What do you think you can do for her?

These three questions refer to the pastoral identity, the pastoral relationship, and the pastoral approach. In recent years, many ministers and priests have been involved in special training programs in order to become more adept at serving the individual needs of other people. Under the guidance of competent supervisors and with the help of new insights in psychodynamics and especially psychotherapy, many have been working hard to make their ministry relevant to men and women struggling with the meaning of their lives and their deaths. But while concentrating on their own identity, or the relationships they have with people and the help they can offer, many ministers and priests begin to realize the far-reaching implications for their own most personal life. It is these implications for the spirituality of the minister that I would like to discuss here.

We will divide this chapter into three parts: Spirituality and the pastoral identity, spirituality and the pastoral relationship, and spirituality and the pastoral approach.

I. Spirituality and the Pastoral Identity

The first question Michael Smith had to face is: "Who am I?" He is not a doctor on the hospital staff who is expected to cure Mrs. Kern of her cancer, he is not a psychologist trained to help Mrs. Kern cope with her anxieties, and he is not a social worker able to see just how far the relationship with her husband and daughter can be of any support to Mrs. Kern. What, then, is his specialty, his own unique contribution, his most personal tool?

The question is a very realistic one in a world that is becoming more and more professional and where one specialty after another is developing. There was a time in which ministers were seen as doctors, psychologists, social workers, and nurses all at once, and in which they were the factotum of the community; centers of knowledge and wisdom. But today many ministers feel that they are amateurs in every field and professional in none. And in the middle of this confusion they often feel very inadequate, suffer from painfully low self-esteem, and doubt if their theology can be made operational to such a degree that people can be helped in an effective way.

It seems that there are two sides to the pastoral identity that demand careful attention:

1. SELF–AFFIRMATION

After the visit to Mrs. Kern, Michael found himself feeling discouraged and guilty. He felt that he had imposed himself on someone who had neither asked for nor wanted his help, and that as a pastor he had failed completely.

Pastors can never live creative, meaningful lives when this feeling becomes predominant. Those who think that they have no special contribution to make to others—that they are seen more as decorations than as important contributors to life, more tolerated than needed—will in the long run become depressed, apathetic, dull, and irritable. Or they will simply decide to leave the ministry to become engaged in what they name a "real" profession.

But where does that leave Mrs. Kern and many people like her? In what kind of condition is a woman who does not want to see her own children when she is dying, who shuns the doctors who try to give her relief, and who asks for a little corner into which she can crawl away like an animal and perish, not wanting anyone to know or see that she, too, does not have her life in her own hands. Neither medicine nor psychology, neither psychiatry nor social work can ever respond to the final question of why human beings come to life, slowly learn to stand, act independently, attach themselves to others, give life to others, and gradually allow others to continue what they started but will not see fulfilled. Those who have not been able to give meaning to their own life cycle and accept it in its terminable reality cannot die as human beings. They have no other way than the way of animals. It was quite understandable that the head of the section where Mrs. Kern stayed asked Michael to go and visit this patient. She knew that Michael could not cure her, but she also realized, perhaps only vaguely, that there is a tremendous difference between dying and slipping away, between giving your life and forsaking it in a hopeless battle, between reaching out to the light that becomes visible in the hour of death and turning away your head and allowing yourself to be drawn into a pit of despair.

Michael might not have been able to make Mrs. Kern's death an act of human surrender, because life perspectives usually don't change in an hour. But he should at least realize that he was indeed asked to save the life of Mrs. Kern—that is, to offer hope that her vulnerability calls forth love in those around her and that her death can also become an ultimate human gift. He might also have made it possible for her husband and children to find hope and strength in that same light dawning in the eyes of their wife and mother as she accepted the truth of her life.

When ministers discover that they really can give life to people by enabling them to face their real life-condition without fear, they will at the same time cease looking at themselves as people on the periphery of reality. Ministers then are right in the center. Many doctors realize how dangerous it is to operate on someone who has no will to live, and many psychologists are humble enough to confess that they cannot give meaning to life and death—even if they might have many insights into the motivations that make people hurt and heal each other. Many sociologists know that no structural changes will make sense as long as it remains unclear where such changes will lead. Thus when we no longer see the meaning of existence, we lose perspective, grasp what is most satisfying to immediate needs, escape in sexual fantasies or drugs, and find life disintegrating to the point of the contemplation of suicide.

Individual pastoral care is in many ways the care most needed and in fact most asked for—at least if we can understand the questions. Pastoral training, therefore, perhaps means first of all the education of pastors so that they might hear questions and become aware of the fact that they are needed more than they realize—that thousands of people are constantly asking life's old question: What is it all about, anyhow? Why should we eat and drink, work and play, raise money and children, and fight constantly a never-ending sequence of frustrations? Or to say it with sages of yore, the Yogavasistha: "What happiness can there be in the world where everyone is born to die?" (cf., W. Allport: *The Individual and his Religion*, Macmillan, 1960, p. 23).

It is on this level that pastors are called to move. And if they become aware of the real questions that are raised right in front of them, they will see that they indeed touch the heart of life. It is then that they cast off their low self-esteem and discover that by affirming the life of their neighbor they are in fact affirming their own ministerial identity.

2. SELF-DENIAL

But at the moment when one might start feeling self-confident or proud, a few disturbing words of Christ come to mind: "For all those wanting to be followers of mine, let them renounce themselves—for those who lose their lives for my sake will find them" (Matthew 16:24–25). Above all, one remembers the almost unbelievable statement of St. Paul: "I live—not with my own life, but with the life of Christ, who lives in me" (Galatians 2:20). Just when ministers might have discovered that they have not only a contribution to make but also the potential to touch the core of life; just when they are ready to affirm themselves and to feel that they are fulfilling their hopes and realizing their deepest aspirations in life, they are faced with the urgent call to deny themselves, to consider themselves servants—useless laborers who are last in line.

Michael put on a white coat so that, like the medical interns, he might be accepted as one of the team. But the fact is that Michael does not really belong to the hospital, does not have any status or medical connection. He is not there to cure Mrs. Kern. In many ways Mike is an outsider who does not know much about illnesses but only about people who happen to be ill. Perhaps his coat is a symbol of his unwillingness to show that he is in fact not part of the hospital team and that he has no medical tools or techniques to offer. Perhaps he is not convinced that he is allowed to come in from the outside only in order to let Mrs. Kern know that although he can do nothing about her cancer, he is nonetheless concerned about the way she is choosing to live out her illness and the way she is choosing to die.

Many ministers and priests seem to be extremely concerned to be *in* with the competent people and to have a clear-cut identity. But is it really so important to come to this professional self-fulfillment? The great influence of Freud, Jung, Rogers, and Frankl is in raising for many ministers the question: How can I be my real self, personal as well as professional? It seems that the clerical waiting list for sensitivity training has become considerably longer than the one for Trappist guesthouses. But is it our vocation to fulfill our own self to its ultimate degree and to create situations in which we can come to what we consider to be the most meaningful, beautiful, and intensive experience?

Thomas Merton, in one of his later works, wrote:

It becomes overwhelmingly important for us to become detached from our everyday conception of ourselves as potential subjects for special unique experiences, or as candidates for realization, attainment and fulfillment. (*Zen and the Birds of Appetite*, New Directions, New York, 1960, p. 76.)

If Mrs. Kern could have profited from Michael's visit, it certainly would not have been because Michael knew a great deal or had answers to the questions of life, but because he was vulnerable and could lose himself for someone else and thereby give her the freedom to talk—not only about her cancer, her problems or present worries, but also about why she was living the way she was and how she was now facing the task of dying.

We can never really minister to our brothers and sisters when we are unwilling to deny ourselves in order to create the space where the God who dwells within us can work. How can we really be of help to others if we keep concentrating on ourselves? How is it that we are so preoccupied with our own lives, our own concerns, and our own interests that we can never really concentrate on the life and plight of another? When will we integrate our preoccupations and give space for the other's pain to enter into us? If we want to fall asleep, for example, we must, in fact, cease concentrating on trying to do so. Only when we endeavor to forget about ourselves for a while can we become really interested in another—that is, concentrate on the experience, the concerns, and the feelings of the one in front of us.

So self-affirmation and self-denial are both parts of the identity of the minister. Are they contrary to each other? The new understanding of Zen Buddhist tradition has certainly made it clear that we feel more at home with the idea of self-fulfillment than with the idea of self-emptying. Dr. H. H. M. Fortmann, the Dutch priest-psychologist, wrote while expecting his own death to come soon:

> . . . the religious problem of the West . . . has to be related to the inflation of the Ego. We have lost the awareness that there is a kind of knowledge, which can only be reached by a reverent process of losing and emptying. (*Oosterse Renaissance*, Ambo Bilthoven, 1970, p. 6.)

Since the East-West dialogue has become a part of many people's lives, especially the young, we have become aware of the fact that there are two forms of consciousness: one that says "be yourself so you can be creative," and the other that says "lose yourself so God can be creative in you." The former stresses individuality, the latter unification.

Pastoral education during recent years has been under the strong influence of Western behavioral sciences. This explains at least part of the emphasis on self and individual creativity. It also makes quite understandable the search for professional identity in the ministry and why it has received so much attention. But if we read certain signs of the times correctly, we discover the growing interest in the way of Siddhartha (the Buddha), so beautifully described by Hermann Hesse, and how this is a powerful suggestion for the pastor of the future. It might well be true that wisdom is coming from the East like the sages who followed the star to find the Christ. If the inflation of the pastor's ego prevents mystical union with God, no Michael can help any Mrs. Kern to make death a final act of surrender.

But self-affirmation and self-emptying are not opposites, because we can never give away what we do not have. We are unable to give ourselves in love when we are not aware of ourselves. We don't ever come to intimacy without having found and claimed our identity. Jesus lived thirty years in a simple family. There He became a man who knew who He was and where He wanted to go. Only then was He ready to empty Himself and give His life for others. His is the way of all ministry. Through long and often painful formation and training, we ministers have to find our place in life, to discover our own contribution, and to affirm our own self: not to cling to it and claim it as our own unique property, but to go out, offer our services to others, and empty ourselves so that God can speak through us and invite others to new life.

So our identity as pastors and ministers, as it becomes visible in our pastoral care, is born from the intangible tension between self-affirmation and self-denial, self-fulfillment and self-emptying, self-realization and self-sacrifice. There are periods in life in which the emphasis is more on one than on the other, but in general it seems that as we become more mature we will become less concerned with girding ourselves and more willing to stretch out our hands and to follow Him who found His life by losing it.

II. Spirituality and the Pastoral Relationship

The growing emphasis on self-denial in the service of the other, besides being crucial for pastoral identity, is also essential to the pastoral relationship. Even if Michael knows quite well what his own role is among the many professionals with whom he is working, the question nonetheless remains: What is his relationship with Mrs. Kern? Mrs. Kern did not ask for him, as was quite obvious from the discussion. And why should Michael knock on the door of a stranger? Does he have that right simply because the head of the section became concerned about a woman's condition? That the doctor visits is understandable, since Mrs. Kern came to the hospital to be treated by doctors. But in allowing herself to be brought to the hospital, Mrs. Kern was certainly not expecting to be visited by a complete stranger affiliated with a religious organization completely alien to her life. Michael was aware of this. He simply said who he was and where he could be reached. He also explained that different religions were represented in the hospital by a minister, a priest, and a rabbi, and that Mrs.

Kern could ask for their services whenever she wanted. Mrs. Kern, however, did not want any service of this kind, and that would have ended the discussion had Michael not shown a little more interest and asked how ill Mrs. Kern had been.

There are two concepts that can help us understand a little better the uniqueness of the pastoral relationship: (1) the concept of the contract, and (2) the concept of the covenant.

1. THE CONTRACT

Many professional relationships between people fail because of an unclear contract. If two people make an appointment with each other, there is a *formal* contract to meet. If one is asking for help and the other is giving help, the *informal* contract is that the problem will be the focus of the meeting. But quite often there is a *secret* contract, which does not always become clear. Sometimes people look for advice but receive a sermon, or they hope to be listened to but get a pep talk, or they seek information but do not hear more than "hm, hm." Within a pastoral relationship between two people many different expectations, which are often the cause of great frustrations, can exist. The fact that Michael was so deeply frustrated that he felt "kicked in the stomach" was obviously related to his wrong expectation that Mrs. Kern would at least be willing to respond to his desire to be of help. And although Mrs. Kern's reaction is quite exceptional, there are many pastors whose unhappiness about their individual pastoral care is directly related to the unclarity of the contract. I remember a woman saying to a pastor: "My boy does not want to go to church anymore. What should I do?"

The pastor said: "You don't quite know how you should react to this new situation, do you?"

The woman said: "Yes, that's what I was trying to say, but what I want to know is what to do."

Here the pastor starts to counsel while the woman wants direct advice. The result, of course, is that the woman goes home unhappy and the pastor feels he did not get anywhere.

People can be helped in many different ways: by support, advice, instruction, a correction, a clarification of feelings, or just simply listening. But they are never helped if they expect one thing and receive another. And the first responsibility of the pastor is to help parishioners become aware of the kind of help they really want and to let them know if he is able to give it to them.

As long as the secret contract remains secret, there is an increased chance that unnecessary disappointments will result. The temptation of many pastors is to become too preoccupied with just one model of personal relationship: pastoral counseling. That model suggests a process in which pastor and parishioner meet in such a way that the parishioner can clarify feelings and mobilize energies so as to find meaning and direction. Often this requires many well-structured meetings, special skills on the part of the pastor, and special attitudes on the part of the parishioner. But this kind of contract is rather rare in a regular parish. More usual are the many short and casual contacts and conversations in the context of which much or little can happen, according to the sensitivity of the pastor.

Some pastors say that they are always busy but have the feeling of never accomplishing anything. This may, of course, be simply the result of poor planning. But when pastors have really found their own identities, they discover at the same time that it is exactly their task to relate to many people in many different ways. It is, in fact, these alternatives of relating that enable them to exercise a ministry that has many forms and many different possibilities. Within this perspective, the desire to have one specialty and to limit oneself to one way of relating is more an escape than a virtue. It is true that this multiformity of the ministry can create great frustration, but this frustration might belong to the essence of the ministry and point to a way of relating that goes beyond the contractual way of the other professions. Let us therefore now look at the concept of the covenant as an important corrective of the contractual view of the pastoral relationship.

2. THE COVENANT

The word "contract," a predominantly economic term, has become a powerful concept in the field of human relationships. The distinction between formal, informal, and secret contracts has helped very much to clarify many failures in professional relationships between people. It is easy to see, therefore, how it has likewise helped many pastors to better understand the different problems as well as possibilities in their relationships with people.

But just as self-affirmation is not the only aspect of the identity of the minister, so "contract" is not the last word about the pastoral relationship. Just as Michael went to see Mrs. Kern even though he was not invited, so too do many ministers and priests knock on doors, ring bells, and walk into houses where nobody is waiting for them. Doctors wouldn't think of going from one house to another to ask if there is anybody ill enough to need help. Psychologists don't call on people to find out if there are emotional problems that will give them a chance to exercise their expertise. But the pastor takes initiatives and can even be considered as an aggressive practitioner who wants "to proclaim the message, welcome or unwelcome, and insist on it" (2 Timothy 4:2).

The fact that the word "contract" cannot really express the pastoral relationship points to the fact that if a pastor likes to consider his relationship with an individual a professional relationship, his profession is of a different kind from all the other helping professions. And here the biblical term "covenant" adds a critical note to the contractual view on the pastoral relationship. The Lord did not establish a contract with the people, but a covenant. A contract ends when one of the partners does not adhere to promises in the agreement. Once a patient no longer pays the doctor, the doctor is free to prefer another patient instead; so, too, when someone does not keep appointments with a psychologist, the psychologist does not feel obligated to reserve further time or to ask why that person did not come. There is indeed an understandable cynicism in the joke that calls a psychiatrist one who is willing to be your friend for one hundred dollars an hour.

But the Lord God says: "Does a woman forget her baby at her breast or fail to cherish the son of her womb? Yes, even if these forget I will never forget you" (Isaiah 49:15). And the one who understands this covenant responds: "If my father and mother desert me, the Lord will care for me still" (Psalms 27:10). In the final analysis, it is not the professional contract but the Divine Covenant that is the basis of a pastoral relationship. In the covenant there is no condition put on faithfulness. It is the unconditional commitment to be of service.

This is perhaps the greatest challenge to everyone who wants to make God's covenant visible in this world: for who does not expect a return for good services? Perhaps we ministers do not ask for money after a pastoral conversation, perhaps we do not even expect a small gift at Christmas or a word of thanks, but can we really detach ourselves from our subtle condition of change? A very good friend of mine, a priest who decided to become a bartender in Amsterdam, said one day: "I don't want to be called 'pastor,' because I've seen too many so-called pastors who are spiritual prostitutes selling their love under the condition of change. If my relationship as pastor is with people affected by the subtle pressure that they should stop drinking so much, get away from drugs, be less promiscuous, cut their long hair, go to court, to church, or the city hall, I am still not really with them but with my own preoccupations, value systems, and expectations, and have made of myself a prostitute and degraded my brothers and sisters by making them victims of my spiritual manipulations." Many ministers complain that nobody says "thanks" to them, that hours spent with people don't bring about any change in the people, that after many years of teaching, preaching, counseling, organizing, and celebrating, people are still apathetic, the church still authoritarian, and the society still corrupt. But if our gratification has to come from visible change, we have made God into a businessman and ourselves into sales managers.

Michael received no thanks for his honest desire to be of help, but even after Mrs. Kern's remark, "I do not care to talk," he said, "Still I would like to drop in from time to time if for no other reason than to say hello, just to see how things are with you." That reaction is quite generous and can hardly be seen as the act of someone looking for gratification. Furthermore, we can nonetheless discover in Michael's awkward approach something of God's faithfulness, which by its incomprehensibility may evoke irritation as well as sympathy.

So we have seen that the pastoral relationship can never be completely understood within the logic of a professional contract. Everyone asks for thanks, hopes for success, and expects change to come about—the minister as much as anyone else. But God did not offer us a contract but a covenant, and challenges those of us who want to make this covenant visible in this world to never make human success a criterion of their love of others.

III. *Spirituality and the Pastoral Approach*

When the identity of the minister is found in the creative tension between self-affirmation and self-denial, and when the nature of the pastoral relationship carries the signs of a professional contract but is ultimately based on the covenant of God and His people, we are left with the question of the pastoral approach. Can anything be said about how ministers or priests should specifically behave when they find themselves in a one-to-one relationship with someone in need of help?

What should Michael have done when he entered Mrs. Kern's room? Was it wrong to start talking about the variety of services the hospital had to offer? Should he have acted differently; said something else, or absolutely nothing? Should he have asked how Mrs. Kern was doing after he had just heard that she was not at all in the mood to talk? These were probably Michael's main problems when he came to his supervisor. He might have said: "Okay, I did a miserable job. I even feel guilty about it, but—can you tell me what I should have done or said?"

Many ministers and priests today take special training exactly because of their need to be more skillful in their individual pastoral relationships. The increasing number of pastoral training centers is witness to the great desire to find an answer to the "how to do it" question. How to have a good conversation with students? How to help someone in a crisis situation? How to relate to the gangsta rapper or the young radical? How to have a meaningful contact with the confused teenager or the rebellious young adult? How to help an embittered dying patient? How to do this and how to do that? Sometimes I have the strange feeling that we are still too preoccupied with the doctor's old problem of how to get the child to swallow the bitter pill. Sweetening the pill, music in the background, or a distracting puppet show? But the pill has to be swallowed. Quite often pastors look to the masters of the behavioral sciences to give them answers for their urgent questions. And many psychologists, sociologists, counselors, and sensitivity trainers become rich today by teaching their ways to eager ministers who admire their skills and hope to find in them a solution for their deep-seated feelings of inadequacy.

I do not want to underestimate the tremendous importance of the great help the social sciences can offer to the pastor. One of the main reasons for great hope in the field of pastoral care is precisely the still-developing dialogue between pastors, sociologists, social workers, psychologists, and psychiatrists. But I also feel that there is a unique dimension to pastoral care that goes beyond professionalism. It is to that dimension that I would like to pay special attention here. I would like to do this by focusing on one specific aspect of many new forms of pastoral training: the writing of the pastoral report.

One of the most important things pastors learn in their training is to write down their experiences. Charles Hall, executive secretary of the Clinical Pastoral Education movement, once said: "What is worth saying is worth writing." If Michael had not written down his painful pastoral visit, he could not have learned much from his experience. But what was there to be learned? I would like to discuss this by using two terms: (1) Role Definition and (2) Contemplation.

1. ROLE DEFINITION

It is no secret that ministers are not accustomed to writing. A good number, of course, boast: "Oh, I could write a book about things that happen in this parish." But very few do. The doctor writes his medical report, the psychologist his test report, the social worker his case report. But most pastors have no document available to help them define their own role. Russel Dicks, one of the pioneers of the clinical training movement, says, "We believe that until the minister develops a method of keeping records of his own with individuals, he has no right to claim a place for himself among the skilled workers in the field of human personality." (*The Art of Ministering to the Sick*, Macmillan, New York, 1936, p. 256.)

By studying the written reports of his pastoral work with individuals, we are able to clarify our own experiences. We also have a concrete way of identifying exactly what happened in our pastoral work and a unique chance to think realistically about alternative ways of pastoral behavior. In this way we are able to define what took place and what has to be done. When Michael looked over the report of his visit to Mrs. Kern, he realized that his nervousness had made him cling to concrete information and behave more like an officer of a tourist bureau than a pastor. He also became aware that he could have prevented much pain if, before the visit, he had asked the doctor or nurse something about Mrs. Kern—her religion and her physical and psychological condition. He started wondering whether his white coat, which of course made him look like a doctor, had not created most of the barrier between them. He was likewise able to think about different ways of relating to an extremely adamant and bitter person, who was unable to face her situation and unable to show her need for human help. So Michael learned from his experience. But "experience" is a very ambivalent word. Many priests, who use their years of experience as an argument for their competence, tend to forget that only a few people learn from experience. One carefully reported and critically evaluated event can often teach someone more than many years filled with experiences empty of understanding. When, however, priests and ministers can define where they stand, they can also draw a map of where they want to go. All professionals are responsible for their own definition. When ministers cannot define their role carefully, they will never be able to make it clear to anyone else. Michael started to define his role when he wrote down his experiences. Perhaps his next visit was a little less frustrating because of it.

But if we look upon role definition as the last word in individual pastoral care, we miss the core of the ministry, which is not skillful practice but reverent contemplation. It would be well, therefore, to finally examine the meaning of contemplation.

2. CONTEMPLATION

The great concern of many supervisors such as Russel Dicks has been to help ministers learn the best response to a given stimulus. Michael's responses to Mrs. Kern's stimuli certainly could have been a lot better. Many alternative responses are imaginable. And although it would be naïve to say that a minister should stay away from all special skills, tools, and techniques in human relationships—we might even wish to have a few more!—skillful responses certainly do not constitute the core of the ministry. Those who write down their experiences not only have a chance to define the event and the best response to it, but also have an invaluable source of theological contemplation. When Anton Boisen, the father of the clinical training movement, asked his students to write down their experiences, he did not think first of all about the "how to do it well" question, but, rather, about the question, "What can I learn from this person whom I meet as a pastor?" For him the most forgotten source of theology was what he called "the living human document." In *The Exploration of the Inner World,* he writes:

> Just as no historian worthy of the name is content to accept on authority the simplified statement of some other histo-rian regarding the problem under investigation, so I have sought to begin not with the ready made formulations contained in books, but with living human documents and with actual social conditions in all their complexities.
> (Harper Torchbooks, New York, p. 135.)

For a person of faith, no meeting is accidental. Mrs. Kern and Michael met. And even though Michael was in no way able to help her as he thought he could, perhaps Mrs. Kern told him something he should never forget: a person can be-come so hard, so bitter, and so disappointed in life that the only wish that remains to that person is to be allowed to crawl into a corner and die like an animal. Mrs. Kern shows in a most naked and terrifying way the condition in which we can find ourselves when we lose faith in the possibility of love.

Michael might have read Kierkegaard, Sartre, Camus, Kafka, and many others who write about anxiety and guilt, loneliness and alienation, sin, and death. But now he stands face to face with someone who says: "You will do me a favor if you leave—and do not return." Michael might have said: "Oh, just another proud and stubborn individual who wants to be left alone"—but then he would not be really contemplating the human condition as it becomes visible in Mrs. Kern's despair.

Mrs. Kern does much more than refuse to talk. She is a living, human document who can give rise to the most fundamental questions of theology: questions of sin and salvation, guilt and forgiveness, isolation and reconciliation, and, finally, of life and death. In her case, however, these questions become more than theoretical—they have immediate implications for the understanding of everyone relating to her: the doctors, whom she could no longer face; her children, whom she refused to see while dying; her husband, who will live on with a memory of an embittered wife; and Michael, who wanted to help her to die but could not.

Pastoral care means much more than pastoral worries. It means a careful and critical contemplation of the human condition. Through this contemplation, pastors can take away the veil and make visible to themselves and to others the fact that good and evil are not just words but visible realities in the life of everyone. In this sense, every pastoral contact is a challenge to understand in a new way God's work with humanity, and to distinguish with a growing sensitivity the light and the darkness in the human heart.

In this way, contemplation is not just an important aspect of the life of the priest or an indispensable condition for a fruitful ministry. Ministry *is* contemplation. It is the ongoing unveiling of reality and the revelation of God's light as well as humanity's darkness. In this perspective, individual pastoral care can never be limited to the application of any skill or technique, since ultimately it is the continuing search for God in the life of the people we want to serve. Indeed, the paradox of the ministry is that we will find the God we want to give in the lives of the people to whom we want to give God.

And so we have seen that if the pastoral approach does not go beyond the level of skills and techniques, we ministers are tempted to become manipulative of others. Only when we learn to see our pastoral relationships as a vital source of theological contemplation can we ourselves also be ministered to by those whom we care for.

Conclusion

The main purpose of this chapter has been to show the implications of individual pastoral care for the personal life of the ministers themselves. I hope that the central movement from professionalism to spirituality has been clear. In the search for professional identity, ministers move from self-affirmation to self-denial; in the establishment of a professional relationship, they move from contract to covenant; and in a professional approach to the individual needs of others, they move from role-definition to contemplation.

If ministers want to be of real help in their contact with people, they have to be professionals with special information, special training, and special skills. But if they want to break through the chains of our manipulative world, they have to move beyond professionalism and, through self-denial and contemplation, become faithful witnesses of God's covenant.

Only Jesus can be called "pastor" in this sense. He cared for many people in their most individual needs. He cared for the woman at the well, for Mary Magdalene, for Nicodemus, and for the men traveling to Emmaus who felt their hearts burn when He talked with them. Jesus was certainly skillful in His relationships with people and was not afraid to use His insights into the stirrings of the human heart. But when asked about the source of His knowledge, He said:

> My teaching is not from myself; it comes from the One who sent me. When a man's doctrine is his own, he is hoping to get honor for himself; but when he is working for the honor of one who sent him, then he is sincere and by no means an impostor. (John 7:16–18)

A minister who cares for people is called to be skillful but not a technician, knowledgeable but not an impostor, professional but not a manipulator. When people are able to deny themselves, to be faithful and to understand the meaning of human suffering, then those who are cared for will discover that God shows divine tender love through the hands of those who want to be of help.

➤

CHAPTER IV

Beyond the Manipulation of Structures

Organizing

The Christian Agent of Social Change

Introduction

When we want to examine the relationship between organizing and spirituality, we can perhaps start nowhere better than with the many painful questions asked by ministers and priests who have become aware of their vocation to be agents of change.

After many hours, days, and years of teaching, preaching, and individual pastoral care, most ministers suddenly stop and ask themselves: Why do I spend so much time in preaching the Word of God while those I really would like to reach are never in my church? Why do I teach children and adults to prepare them for a society that for many does not offer even the possibility of living the life I am trying to advocate? Why do I call people together to celebrate their unity while they are not able to live together in peace but are torn apart by hate, competition, and segregation? Why do I spend so many hours talking about the individual pains of people, while I leave the society that creates these pains unchanged?

There is a growing frustration in the life of many ministers and priests because of the awareness that their everyday work does not really touch the structures of life. They feel like people who help the wounded but are unable to stop the war. Their words in the pulpit, the classroom, and the rectory may be a support to many people and give them the courage to face their lives again, but what about the sick society itself, suffering from war, pollution, poverty, crimes, and violence? When there is something basically wrong with the world in which we live, what help are all our words?

Is it our task to help people adapt to a society that is not worth adapting to? What does it mean to talk to a woman who does not have enough bread for her children? No counseling skill will take away their hunger. What does it mean to preach love and understanding in a community where people have no decent houses to live in, no jobs in which to earn a living; where children have no space to play, and where most people have lost faith in the words of those who announce a better world to come?

More and more ministers and priests are haunted by these questions and wonder if the church has not in fact moved away to the periphery of life and, although still caring for people, has failed to change the structures of society itself in order to make a real Christian life possible.

Over the last few years, this awareness has grown, and many ministers and priests are wondering if it is really possible to become agents of social change; to extend their pastoral care not only to individuals but to social structures as well. New training centers have developed, such as the Ecumenical Insitute and the Urban Training Center in Chicago. In such places the first question is not: How can I help this individual who has a problem, but: How can I help this society change so that fewer people have problems? The focus is not so much on the pastoral relationship and the pastoral approach, but on the careful analysis of the social situation, the definition of the specific issue at hand, the inventory of the sources of the community, and the development of a careful strategy to bring about social change.

But what is the task of the minister and priest in the complex field of community organization? When that term suggests that it is the task of ministers to take all the responsibility for many specific projects into their own hands, I certainly would say No, but when it indicates the vocation to make people aware of their hidden potential, to unify the many different self-interests into a common concern, to remove the paralyzing influence of fatalism, and to offer a vision that makes people see their social responsibility and strive beyond the many concrete actions to a Christian community in faith, then they might very well consider themselves to be organizers in a unique way. They can awaken the dormant powers in their milieu. They can break through the chains of pessimism and collective depression and make their people aware that things do not necessarily have to be the way they are. They can prevent people from falling back in apathy after unexpected disappointments, and from using destructive escapisms instead of constructive action. They can help create a mentality of hope and confidence, which makes a community flexible and adaptable to new situations and always alert for new possibilities and new perspectives.

In this sense, a minister or priest can be an agent of social change without having to be trapped in the pitfalls of a manipulative world. But this requires a spirituality, a way of living that allows us to be very much involved in this world precisely because we are free toward it and do not cling to it with a destructive possessiveness. To describe this spirituality, we first have to identify the different dangers to which we are exposed in our social activities. Therefore, I will divide this

chapter into two parts: (1) the pitfalls of the organizer, and
(2) the Christian agent of social change.

I. The Pitfalls of the Organizer

When we ask people about the condition of our world today, we quickly become aware that many of them have come
to the conclusion that our society is so completely rotten and
its structures so totally failed that the only solution to the
problem is a total structural and social change. They are willing to fight for it and do anything possible to make this new
society come about. They have become aware that the slogan
"Change the world by beginning with yourself" does not
work, and that, rather, if one truly wants to change, then the
world in which one lives has to change first. They feel that
changing people without changing the structures is a waste of
time, and that real change has to come from the outside, even
if violence, cruelty, and execution have to be used to bring it
about. This is the attitude of the commissar of the Russian
Revolution as described by Arthur Koestler (*The Yogi and the
Commissar*, Collier Books, New York, 1945). This is also the
attitude of those many revolutionaries today who burn banks,
destroy property, start street fights, and do everything possible
to upset the existing order in the conviction that the new
world will be born out of the ashes of the old. There are probably very few ministers and priests who share this conviction,
with all its consequences. However, many of them, who have
become deeply aware of the overwhelming problems of our
society, might nonetheless be inclined to suggest tactics and
strategies that are still based on the supposition that humans
will only change if the structures change first.

It seems to me that there are three pitfalls, three dangers, that threaten this type of social activism: concretism, power, and pride.

1. THE DANGER OF CONCRETISM

The danger of concretism is the inclination to make very concrete and specific results the main motivation for continuing social action. Many times it seems that much of the suffering and frustration of people working in ghettos, slums, or other underdeveloped areas is the result of the fact that the changes they hoped to accomplish did not come about. They start their work with great enthusiasm and generous willingness to be of help, but after a few years, when they see that the situation is still essentially the same as when they started, they leave disappointed and sometimes bitter, hurt by a loss of self-esteem and feelings of failure and worthlessness. Not a few Peace Corps workers, Vista workers, and Papal Volunteers can attest to this experience.

Quite often the reason for this attitude is that these people enter their work with preconceived ideas about how things should be, as if they were saying: "*This* is what these people need"—better houses, better education, better recreation facilities, better sewer systems, labor unions, cooperatives, et cetera. But these very specific aims might well ruin their effectiveness, make them blind to what people really need and deaf to what they say. So, often, totally in contrast with their desire, they create hostility in the people they want to help.

I remember once working in a very poor Dutch neighborhood. I visited a family with ten children who were walking around in rags during the day and sleeping together in three large old beds at night. I felt that the help they needed was obvious. I ordered some clothes and bought a few more beds. But later, when I entered the house unexpectedly, there was a

big party going on with beer and cakes. My good friends had
sold the beds and most of the clothes in order to invite their
friends and neighbors in to celebrate the birthday of their el-
dest son. Actually, they had enough clothes—though they
didn't know how to repair them—and sleeping in a separate
bed seemed quite lonely for most of the children.

It is obvious that my help was more an expression of what
I thought a good life ought to be rather than what they
thought about it. This same kind of mistake is made in many
situations. New houses, for example, are given to people by
others who do not realize that living in a new house might not
be nearly as important as living close to one's friends.

A good number of population programs have totally failed
because well-meaning helpers were handing out their new
technological inventions—pills, IUDs, and other contracep-
tives—without carefully asking themselves how people feel
about having large families, what it means to a couple to have
none or only a few children, and how other populations judge
the values of life. Quite often, sex education has been considered a solution to problems without a careful study of the
motivation of people's sexual behavior, and new expensive
programs have been endorsed as if all people think, feel,
and act alike. In short, our own preconceived, concretionary
views have caused more hindrance than assistance in our attempts to improve our world and help one another.

2. THE DANGER OF POWER

People who organize are in constant danger of creating
small kingdoms for themselves. It is extremely difficult to take
initiatives and develop new plans without claiming the result
as something that is yours. Just as many parents find it hard to
let their children choose their own lifestyles, so too do many

"organizing priests" want to keep running the show and telling people what to do.

One way of exercising power over people is to become subject to what Dr. John Santos, head of the psychology department at the University of Notre Dame, calls the education-enlightenment hypothesis—that is, the hypothesis that makes us think that if we tell people what makes good sense to us, it will automatically make good sense to them as well. Many social reformers still think that when you give people the right information and the right instructions they will become so enlightened that they will do exactly what you have in mind. But people do not always feel that those things you consider to be good for them necessarily are so. Many well-intentioned projects written up by many well-educated people have been ignored and even ridiculed by those who have other values and perspectives. While you think a hundred-dollar bill is worth much, someone else might just light his cigarette with it. Education itself can become a form of power when we think that we are helping people by presenting them with our value system as the ideal way of life. The Black Power movement was, in part, a reaction against the education-enlightenment hypothesis that made us think that blacks would be much happier if they were allowed to share in whites' way of life. But, in fact, this only means that education has become propaganda and that offering help has become part of the power game.

The most subtle desire for power, and the most difficult to overcome, is the desire for thanks. As long as people keep thanking us for what we have done for them, they are, in effect, admitting that they were at least for some time dependent upon us. And it is perhaps exactly for this reason that we find in areas where people are living in very poor conditions a certain resistance against explicit thankfulness. Nobody likes to be considered in need of help or not able—facts which an expression of thanks often explicitly asserts. It should therefore come as no surprise that many men and women who have spent many days helping others seldom hear a word of thanks. In such cases, such words would only be reminders of dependency and threats to self-respect. Not only individuals but even whole countries have thus refused gifts of money and badly needed medicine because they preferred to die with what self-respect they had rather than to live with the feeling that others have to keep them on their feet.

But for those who are aware of the needs of other people and want to do something about them, it is difficult to live without at least a small kingdom of thankful people who are willing to say that without them they would not be who they are now or do what they do now.

3. THE DANGER OF PRIDE

Finally, there is the great temptation of pride. All those who want to change society are in danger of putting themselves above that society and being more conscious of the weaknesses of others than of the weakness in their own souls. Reformers, who are convinced that things have to become different, are out to convert the world but are tempted at the same time to think that they themselves do not need conversion. Instead of seeing themselves as full members of that same society which needs reform, they may approach it with the fantasy of being untouchable redeemers who themselves are always right and just.

They might see the cruel segregation between races but be blind to the fact that what they see happening dramatically on the world scene is also happening in themselves when they condemn certain people as being stupid, others as being narrow-minded, and still others as being conceited. They might be very critical of capitalism and the waste of money but not see that their own style of life would be impossible without the capitalistic society that they condemn. They might feel that many people should have a better life and more human respect but at the same time be unable to listen to people, accept their criticism, and believe that they can learn from them. They might always be busy going from one meeting to another and forget that they themselves tend to lose contact with the sources of their own existence and become deaf to the voice that calls from within. They might even be afraid to be alone and face the fact that they themselves are in just as much need of change as is the world they want to convert.

The three dangers for everyone who is concerned about social change are, therefore, concretism, power, and pride. When Jesus had become aware of His vocation to criticize the society in which He lived, to question its basic supposition, and to work for the Kingdom to come, He knew that He too could have become another organizer in the long line of those who had already called themselves Messiahs. And indeed, He was tempted to bring about immediate results and change the stones into bread, to take the power and the glory of all the kingdoms of the world, and to prove His invulnerability by throwing Himself down from the parapet of the temple and allowing the angels to guard Him.

But only through overcoming these temptations could He become a revolutionary who was able to break through the narrowing chains of His world and surpass all political ambitions in order to make visible the new Kingdom to come. In this sense, Herbert McCabe is right when he says:

The likeliest model for the Christian minister—is the revolutionary leader; indeed, the priest should be a revolutionary leader, but one who goes in and through what
in today's terms is called a political revolution to a depth
which today we call metaphysical or spiritual. This inter-
pretation of the revolution in its ultimate depths *is* the
proclamation of the gospel. (*Priesthood and Revolution*, Com-
monweal, September 20, 1968, p. 626.)

We are now ready to ask ourselves what the main traits are
of the one who wants to be a Christian agent of social change.

II. The Christian Agent of Social Change

Everyone who has become aware of the illnesses of the society in which we live and who feels a growing need to work
for social change is faced with the temptations of concretism,
power, and pride. And many have become so deeply impressed by these temptations that they do not see how to avoid
them. It almost seems that being both an agent for social
change and a Christian becomes a contradiction. Many ask
themselves: How can I work for a better world without being
tempted to conspiracy, gossip, and hatred? How can I work for
the deprived black man without sharing his hostile feelings
for the white? How can I help the poor without hating
those whom I see as their exploiters? How can I criticize the
Establishment without being conceited, self-righteous, and
close-minded? In short, how can I actively work for a better
world and not harm the Christian values that tell me to love
my enemies as well as my friends?

Many people who become hurt in this struggle for social
reform have indeed become so overwhelmed by this problem

that in order to avoid becoming like the commissar who was willing to sacrifice the individual to change the structure, they choose what is in effect the opposite way: the way of the yogi. It is not difficult to understand why many people, tired by social action and disappointed with its results, have chosen the inward way. All over the country we see new centers of meditation and concentration in which people try to come to terms with this chaotic world by changing the world from within and making themselves internally free. Quite often they have turned to the East to find a new way. Many have become so deeply convinced that all the conflicts of the world find their origins in the human heart and that their internal life is just a miniature of the cruel battlefields of the large society, that for them the only real place to start changing the world is to start in the center of their own inner life.

Arthur Koestler writes: "The Yogi believes that nothing can be changed by external organisations, but everything by the individual attempt from within, and that everyone who thinks otherwise escapes the real problem." (*The Yogi and the Commissar*)

It might be worthwhile to ask if the growing interest in the Pentecostal movement within the Catholic Church is not in some way an expression of this same attitude. By concentration on inner conversion and the eradication of evil from the human heart, by stressing personal love and the creation of small communities of prayer, many deeply committed Pentecostals are basically saying that the only way to change our destructive world is to start with a change in one's heart. It is not surprising, therefore, to find that the Pentecostals, like the yogi, have *often* been accused of being aloof and indifferent to the great social problems of war, poverty, pollution, segregation, social injustice, and crime, and of having escaped into a personal garden where they can concentrate on their own souls, experience the stirrings of the Spirit, and make their own conversion the criterion for the solutions of the problems of this world.

But neither the commissar nor the yogi, neither the radical Christian reformer nor the Pentecostal is able to solve the problems of our society. The great task of ministry, rather, is to live and to help live in the tension between both and to search for a synthesis. Christian agents of social change are called upon to be social reformers who do not lose their own souls, to be active and prayerful at the same time. They are called upon to be concerned with the large issues of our time without losing sight of the children, the poor, the sick, and the old, who ask for our personal care and attention. In a Christian perspective, this careful balance becomes a possibility. Living in this perspective and opening it for the members of their own community, ministers become true agents of social change. And we can even say that insofar as Christians make this perspective visible, they in fact become ministers. I would, therefore, like now to describe this perspective as one of hope, of creative receptivity, and of shared responsibility.

1. THE PERSPECTIVE OF HOPE

Gabriel Marcel has made it clear that what many people call "hope" is in fact a form of wish-fulfillment thinking. The life of anyone is filled with wishes. A child wishes for a bicycle, a boy wishes for a football, a student wishes for a good grade, a man wishes for a car, a house, a job. A sick man wishes to be cured; a poor woman, to become rich; a prisoner, to become free. This wish-fulfillment thinking is like waiting for a Santa Claus whose task it is to satisfy very specific needs and desires—immediately, if possible. When our lives are filled with this type of specific concrete wish, however, we are in constant danger of becoming disappointed, bitter, angry, or indifferent, since more often than not our wishes don't come true, and we come to feel that somewhere and somehow we have been betrayed.

I have the feeling that many ministers and priests working for social change are often the victims of this wish-fulfillment thinking. They work for better housing, better schools, or a better neighborhood. They have very concrete goals in mind and very specific ways to realize them. But although the goals are important and the means reasonable, they tend, nonetheless, to make the fulfillment of their wishes the criterion for their own self-esteem. Basically, they are still people of little faith, who are more concerned with the gift they want than the giver from whom they want it.

Only through hope are we able to overcome this concretionary attitude, for hope is not directed to the gift but to the Giver of all gifts. We wish *that*, but we hope *in* (see Paul Pruyser, *A Dynamic Psychology of Religion,* Harper & Row, 1968, pp. 166–170). Essential to hope, therefore, is that we do not ask for guarantees; that we do not put conditions on our actions; that we do not ask for insurance, but expect everything from others without putting any limit on our trust. Perhaps the best example of a hopeful attitude is still the attitude of a little boy toward his mother. He is constantly asking for very concrete things, but his love for his mother does not depend upon the fulfillment of these wishes. The child knows that the mother wants the best for him—although he might cry or even be very angry at times, he keeps living in the conviction that his mother wants only what is good for him.

Those who work for social change usually have very specific things in mind, as they must, but they can only remain

people of faith when they view every result they have
achieved as a gift to be accepted in freedom. Nobody can
force the soul of a community. The only possibility open is to
create conditions in which the community can freely develop
and discover the ways that lead to redemption.

People of hope can give all their energy, time, and abilities
to the people they work for, but when they attach themselves
to any specific result they can lose sight of their ultimate objective. Through the attitude of hope, agents of social change
do not fall into the temptation of concretism. They do not
worry about the results of their work, because they believe
that God will fulfill all promises and that it is only a temptation to want to know exactly how this will happen. In the
same way, a man and a woman who promise faithfulness to
each other do not want to know how things will look twenty
years later. Only when they leave their future open can they
prevent disappointments and receive the results of their mutual relationship as a gift.

When Christians can offer this perspective of hope, they
free us to look beyond the immediate needs of the community and understand our activities in a larger perspective.
Perhaps there is no better example of this type of leadership
than that given by Martin Luther King. He stimulated his people to work for very concrete rights—an equal place on the
bus and in the restaurant, and an equal right to vote—but at
the same time he never made this an ultimate value but always
looked beyond the results of his actions to the larger issue involved: the total freedom of the human person. Therefore, he
could say that not only are the blacks unfree, but so are the
whites who suppress them. Therefore, he could prevent people from using violence when a desired goal was not accomplished. Therefore, he could give himself totally to the cause

of civil rights even while knowing that he would not see the results. Therefore, he was not afraid of death. In the midst of all activities, he kept reminding his people that although few wishes were fulfilled and few changes brought about, there was no reason for despair. He kept reminding his followers that they were on the road to the promised land and that they had to cross the desert first to reach the place where God would make all people free. Martin Luther King was able to exercise such a powerful spiritual leadership because, although he asked for freedom NOW, he had learned to be patient and wait until God's will fulfilled every one of God's promises.

2. THE PERSPECTIVE OF CREATIVE RECEPTIVITY

By developing in themselves and others the willingness to receive, ministers can prevent human beings from falling into the temptation of power. We who want to bring about change have first of all to learn to be changed by those whom we want to help. This, of course, is exceptionally difficult for those who are undergoing their first exposure to an area of distress. They see poor houses, hungry people, dirty streets; they hear people cry in pain without medical care, smell un-washed bodies, and in general are overwhelmed by the misery all around them. But none of us will be able to really give if we have not discovered that what we give is only a small thing compared to what we have received. When Jesus says: "Happy the poor, the hungry, and the weeping" (Luke 6:21), we have to be able to *see* that happiness. When Jesus says: "What you did to the least of my brothers, you did to me" (Matthew 25:40), he is addressing to us a direct invitation not only to help but also to discover the beauty of God in those who are to be helped. As long as we see only distasteful poverty, we are not really entitled to give. When, however, we find people who have truly devoted themselves to work in the slums and the ghettos and who feel that their vocation is to be of service there, we find that they have discovered that in the smiles of the children, the hospitality of the people; in the expressions they use, the stories they tell, the wisdom they show, the goods they share; there is hidden so much richness and beauty, so much affection and human warmth, that the work they are doing is only a small return for what they have already received. In this respect we can better understand those many missionaries who, after living for years in the poorest circumstances, nonetheless became homesick for their missions as soon as they returned to their affluent countries. It was not because they wanted to suffer more, but because they had found a beauty in their people that they missed in their home communities.

There are many countries, cities, and neighborhoods that need help, and it is sad to see that we still believe that the best way to motivate others to offer their assistance is to show through books and photographs how inhumanely these people have to live. This certainly creates enough feelings of guilt to make people open their wallets and give some money, thereby soothing their consciences for a while. But this is not a Christian response. That the exposure of misery can evoke not only pity but also aggression has become quite clear in concentration camps, in films about starving children in Ethiopia, and in the endless exposure of emaciated bodies by TV, radio, and newspaper. As long as we want to change the condition of other people because we feel guilty about our wealth, we are still playing the power game and waiting for thanks. But when we start discovering that in many ways we are the poor and those who need our help are the wealthy, who have a lot to give, we become true social agents and do not give in to the temptation of power, because we have discovered that our task is not a heavy burden or a brave sacrifice but an opportunity to see more and more of the face of Him whom we want to meet. I wish that more books were written about the so-called "poor" countries and "poor" cities, not only to show how poor they are and how much help they need, but also to show the beauty of their lives, their sayings, their customs, their way of life. Perhaps a new form of Christian "tourism" could then develop in which those who travel can enrich their lives with the wisdom, knowledge, and experience of their hosts.

3. THE PERSPECTIVE OF SHARED RESPONSIBILITY

When we think about leaders, we still tend to think of individuals with special talents. And indeed, when we think of Pope John Paul II, John F. Kennedy, Martin Luther King, and Dag Hammarskjöld, we easily realize that they were agents of social change with exceptional influence on the lives of many people—even on the course of history. But it would be a mistake to keep waiting for people like them to do the great things. Not too long ago, I talked with a black sociologist and asked him about the leadership in the black community. He said: "Perhaps we needed men like King, but now more than ever it is important to look not so much for individuals as for communities which are able to bring about change."

If Christian laypeople, ministers, and priests really want to be agents of social change, the first thing they have to learn is how to share leadership. We are used to saying to people that they have responsibilities. To say that they also have the authority that goes with it, however, is something else. It is amazing to find that most priests are still working very much on their own and have not yet found the creative ways to mobilize the potential leadership in their parishes and share their responsibilities with others.

First of all, there is the fact that there are still only a few parishes where priests really know what the others are doing. While no hospital or school can function without regular staff conferences, it is still a rare exception to see parishes where the common concerns are regularly discussed, analyzed, and evaluated, and where there is any kind of strategy or long-range planning. Secondly, the laity are rarely, if ever, invited to participate in the pastoral work. At the same time, when ministers are busy complaining that they are overworked with visiting the sick and the old, directing meetings, taking care of the finances, and other odds and ends, they are also failing to realize that real leadership means a delegation of tasks. Thirdly, no parish in any city can be considered as its own little kingdom. When pastors and people from different parishes can come together regularly, discuss their common problems, utilize each other's talents, exchange ideas, unite projects, and work out common plans in terms of teaching, preaching, pastoral care, and financing; when they can critically evaluate the main problems of their city, raise their voices together when needed, and let the people know that the Christian community is deeply concerned about the crucial issues of the day, then the church cannot be ignored, and although a great deal of irritation and even open hostility might be the result, we could at least then be certain that God's Word is again a word that must be taken seriously.

The problem of pride, of course, still remains. The remark "mind your own business" can also be heard in the mouths of many Christians. It is not easy to say that you cannot do something yourself, that you are in need of constant criticism, that you are willing to be reminded that the problems of the society are also part of your problems. But whenever pastoral workers, ministers, priests, and laypeople come together in a spirit of charity and humility, new things will start happening.

These pastoral staff meetings can, of course, easily be misunderstood as meetings in the spirit of the commissar, with the primary purpose of working out strategies and planning careful attacks on social problems. But it does not have to be that way. In the middle of a *poblacion* in Santiago, where poverty, hunger, and misery are all around, priests and sisters nonetheless come together for many hours a week, not primarily to formulate a plan of action, but to share each other's experiences, to carefully contemplate the reality in which they live, to make each other see why people do what they do and say what they say, and to celebrate the Eucharist together as a thanksgiving for being allowed to be of service to the people. Outsiders might, of course, say: "Why don't you go to work, why do you spend so much time together when there are still so many people who do not have enough to eat and to drink?" But these men and women know that to be real agents of change they have to be contemplatives at heart, able to hear the voice of God in the middle of the crying children, and see God's face behind the dirty curtain of misery.

We have now seen how the perspective of hope prevents us from being tempted to look for immediate results, how it can help us avoid the pitfalls of power through the perspective of receptivity, and how it can temper individual pride by a shared responsibility that allows mutual criticism as well as mutual support.

Through living in these perspectives, ministers can become catalysts; that is, persons who can uncover the hidden potentials of their community and channel them into creative social action.

Conclusion

The general question of this chapter was: What is the relationship between spirituality and organization? This question led us to the more specific problem: How can ministers be real agents of social change? We discussed the attitude of the commissar, who wants to change the structures first—even if he has to use power and sacrifice people to come to the concrete results he thinks are indispensable for the new world to come. We also discussed the attitude of the inward-looking person, who feels that only by changing the hearts of the individual can we change the structures of our society. But just as the social activist is in danger of forgetting that the pains of our society are also to be found in the heart of the reformer, so too does the inward-looking person easily overlook the colossal problems of our society that go far beyond the personal insights of any individual. But anyone who wants to be an agent of social change is constantly challenged to look for the creative synthesis between the social activist and the inward-looking person. To avoid concretism, power, and pride, we have to live in the perspectives of hope, receptivity, and shared responsibility—all of which means that we must be contemplative. Christian life is not a life divided between times for action and times for contemplation. No. Real social action is a way of contemplation, and real contemplation is the core of social action. In the final analysis, action and contemplation are two sides of the same reality that makes us agents of change. Only the synthesis between the commissar and the yogi makes it possible, therefore, to be real agents of social change and to avoid the traps of manipulation. Only this synthesis allows us to look beyond all political, social, and economic developments in order to keep us forever awake and always waiting for a new world to come. For Christians are only Christians when they unceasingly ask critical questions of the society in which they live and continuously stress the necessity for conversion, not only of the individual but also of the world. We are only Christian when we refuse to allow ourselves or anyone else to settle into a comfortable rest. We must remain dissatisfied with the status quo. And we believe that we have an essential role to play in the realization of the new world to come—even if we cannot say how that world will come about. We are only Christian when we keep saying to everyone we meet that the Good News of the Reign of God has to be proclaimed to the whole world and witnessed to all nations (Matthew 24:13). As long as we are alive, we must keep searching for a new order without divisions between people, for a new structure that allows every person to shake hands with every other person, and for a new life in which there will be everlasting unity and peace. We must not allow our neighbors to stop moving, to lose courage, or to escape into small, everyday pleasures to which they can cling. We must be irritated by satisfaction and self-contentment in ourselves as well as in others, since we know with an unshakable certainty that something great is coming of which we have already seen the first rays of light. We must believe that this world not only passes but has to pass in order to let the new world be born. We must believe that there will never be a moment in this life in which we can rest in the supposition that there is nothing left to do. But we will not despair when we do not see the result we have wanted to see. For in the midst of all this work, we keep hearing the words of the One sitting on the throne: "I am making the whole of creation new" (Revelation 21:5).

➤

CHAPTER V

Beyond the Protective Ritual

Celebrating

Obedient Acceptance of Life

Introduction

In January of 1970, students of the Perkins School of Theology in Dallas, Texas, met for an inter-term seminar on the Cultural Revolution and the Church. At the end of the course, prepared by the Ecumenical Institute in Chicago, they composed what can be considered a common creed. In that creed they wrote the following remarkable words:

> Standing before the mystery—man discovers that he has but one life to live—his own. To accept that fact, and to live it, is to receive grace and to discover that all of life is good. And when we die to our illusions that life is any other way than that, we discover the secret of all life: to die is to live. We are those who name this happening the Jesus Christ Event and reclaim for our time the message of the Biblical people. (Bimonthly Newsletter of the Ecumenical Institute, Vol. IV, No. 3, Jan–Feb. 1970, p. 3.)

This powerful expression of faith makes it clear that ministers are those who challenge us to *celebrate life*; that is, to turn away from fatalism and despair and to make our discovery that we have but one life to live into an ongoing recognition of God's work within us. But how can this celebration really be a human possibility? Our lives vibrate between two darknesses. We hesitantly come forth out of the darkness of birth and slowly vanish into the darkness of death. We move from dust to dust, from unknown to unknown, from mystery to mystery. We try to keep a vital balance on the thin rope that is stretched between two definitive endings that we have never seen or understood. We are surrounded by the reality of the unseen, which fills every part of our life with a moment of terror but at the same time holds the secret mystery of our being alive.

The Christian minister is the one whose vocation is to make it possible for us not only to fully face our human situation but also to celebrate it in all its awesome reality.

But how do we celebrate life when we understand neither its ultimate boundaries nor the full meaning of what happens between them? Celebration seems the least appropriate response to our ambiguous condition. And if we want to celebrate, what kind of person can show us the way in which to realize our desires? These questions are essential to any attempt to discover the relationship between celebrating and spirituality. Therefore in this chapter I want to raise two questions: (1) how do we celebrate life? and (2) what kind of person helps us to celebrate?

I. How Do We Celebrate Life?

When we speak about celebration, we tend rather easily to bring to mind happy, pleasant, gay festivities in which we can forget for a while the hardships of life and immerse ourselves in an atmosphere of music, dance, drinks, laughter, and a lot of cozy small-talk. But celebration in the Christian sense has very little to do with any of this. Celebration is only possible through the deep realization that life and death are never found completely separate. Celebration can only really come about where fear and love, joy and sorrow, tears and smiles can exist together. Celebration is the acceptance of life in a constantly increasing awareness of its preciousness. And life is precious not only because it can be seen, touched, and tasted, but also because it will be gone one day. When we celebrate a wedding, we celebrate a union as well as a departure; when we celebrate death, we celebrate lost friendship as well as gained liberty. There can be tears after weddings and smiles after funerals. We can indeed make our sorrows, just as much as our joys, part of our celebration of life in the deep realization that life and death are not opponents but do, in fact, kiss each other at every moment of our existence. When we are born, we become free to breathe on our own but lose the safety of our mother's body; when we go to school, we are free to join a greater society but lose a particular place in our family; when we marry, we find a new partner but lose the special tie we had with our parents; when we find work, we win our independence by making our own money but lose the stimulation of teachers and fellow students; when we receive children, we discover a new world but lose much of our freedom to move; when we are promoted, we become more important in the eyes of others but lose the chance to take many risks; when we retire, we finally have the chance to do what we wanted but lose the support of being wanted. When we have been able to celebrate life in all of these decisive moments where gaining and losing—that is, life and death—touched each other all the time, we will be able to celebrate even our own dying because we have learned from life that only we who lose our lives can find them (cf. Matthew 16:25).

Those who are able to celebrate life can prevent the temp-

tation to search for clean joy or clean sorrow. Life is not
wrapped in cellophane and protected against all infections.
Celebration is the opposite of an escape from the realities of
the full acceptance of life in its total complexity. If we now ask
ourselves what the meaning of this acceptance is, we have to
look at three main components of the act of accepting: affirming, remembering, and expecting.

1. AFFIRMING

Celebrating is first of all the full affirmation of our present
condition. We say with full consciousness: We are, we are
here, we are now, and let it be that way. We can only really
celebrate when we are present in the present. If anything has
become clear, it is that we have to a large extent lost the ca-
pability to live in the present. Many so-called celebrations are
not much more than painful moments between bothersome
preparations and boring after-talks. We can only celebrate if
there *is* something present that can be celebrated. We cannot
celebrate Christmas when there is nothing new born here and
now, we cannot celebrate Easter when no new life becomes
visible, we cannot celebrate Pentecost when there is no Spirit
whatsoever to celebrate. Celebration is the recognition that
something is there and needs to be made visible so that we can
all say Yes to it.

I found a beautiful illustration of this in the meditation ses-
sions of the members of the so-called *now generation*. Young
people come together and for hours try to become present to
each other and to recognize their togetherness as a precious
reality. But how difficult this is! You can hardly take one step,
one breath, without being flooded by thoughts and ideas that
pull you away from yourself here and now and make you
worry about thousands of little things. You find yourself

thinking about your unfinished paper, your plans for tomorrow, or your last conversation. You find yourself asking thousands of unanswerable questions and looking at thousands of invisible pictures. You are not where you are but somewhere where you do not want to be. But when you become able, slowly and carefully, to push all these unwelcome intruders away from your mind, you become aware that there has been something waiting for you of which you had not been aware, and that you really can become present to your own self. At the same time, you also become aware of the real presence of others who are with you, because, since they know that their experience will find resonance in yours, they are willing to show you what they have discovered in their own presence.

In this context it becomes clear what praying together really means. It does not mean worrying together, but rather becoming present for each other in a very real way. Then it becomes possible to share ideas, because they are really ours; to communicate feelings, because they are actually there; to talk about concerns, because they hurt us and we feel their pains in our own soul. Then the formulation of intentions is much more than an at-random choice from among the many possible problems we can think of. It becomes, rather, an attempt to be visible and available to each other just as we are at this very moment. What we then ask from each other is not, first of all, to solve a problem or to give a hand, but to affirm each other in the many different ways we experience life. When this takes place, community starts to form and becomes a reality that can be celebrated as an affirmation of the multiformity of being in which we all take part.

2. REMEMBERING

But people cannot really celebrate their lives in the present when they are not meaningfully related to the past. The present cannot be experienced as present if the past cannot be remembered as past. People without a past cannot celebrate the present and accept their lives as their own.

Not too long ago I picked up a hitchhiker who told me that after a serious accident he had lost his memory of all the things that had happened to him during the last ten years. When he came back to the town where he had lived, everything was new for him; no feelings, ideas, or associations were connected with the houses he saw and the streets he walked on. His friends had become strangers to him, and the things he had done had lost all their connections with his past. He had become a man without a history and, therefore, a man who could no longer give meaning to his present experience.

The way people relate to their own past is of crucial importance for their life-experience. The past can become a prison in which you feel you are caught forever, or a constant reason to compliment yourself. Your past can make you deeply ashamed or guilt-ridden, but it can also be the cause of pride and self-contentment. Some people will say with remorse: "If I could live my life again, I certainly would do it differently"; others will say with self-assertion: "You might think I am an old, weak man, but look at those trophies there; I won those when I was young." Memory is one of the greatest sources of human happiness and human suffering. If we want to celebrate our lives in the present, we cannot cut ourselves off from our past. We are instead invited to look at our history as the sequence of events that brought us to where we are now and that help us to understand what it means to be here at this moment in this world.

Those who celebrate life will not make their past into a

prison or a source of pride, but will face the facts of history and fully accept them as the elements that allow us to claim our experiences as our own.

When we commemorate during a liturgical celebration those who have gone before us, we do much more than direct a pious thought to our deceased family and friends; we recognize that we stand in the midst of history, and that the affirmation of our present condition is grounded in the recognition that we were brought to where we are now by the innumerable people who lived *their* lives before we were given the chance to live *ours*.

3. EXPECTING

But besides affirming life and remembering it, celebration is filled with expectations for the future. If the past had the last word, we would imprison ourselves more and more the older we became. If the present were the ultimate moment of satisfaction, we would cling to it with a hedonistic eagerness, trying to squeeze the last drop of life out of it. But the present holds promises and reaches out to the horizons of life, and this makes it possible for us to embrace our future as well as our past in the moment of celebration.

The truth of this was brought home very forcefully to me by a painful experience. A friend of mine died in Tunisia, where she had gone to work for a few months to help the people who suffered from a terrible flood. Her parents, simple farmers living in a small village, expected much from their daughter, who had been the first university student in the family. Her death in a distant country unknown to most of the people of the village paralyzed her family and friends and came as a shock to the entire town.

The most horrible week was the week when there was nothing but the telegram, that ridiculous piece of paper saying what could not be believed. But when the body was flown back and brought into the village, the death of this student could be celebrated. The fact that she had died while really doing good could be affirmed, and her past could be remembered as a chain of events that had led to the tragic accident. But I am deeply convinced that it became a real celebration only because of the fact that new life became visible around the body of this young woman. Suddenly people realized what it meant to give one's life for others; men and women who never had heard about Tunisia started to talk about it and to ask what kind of people those strange-looking Muslims really were. People from the city met people from the village and became friends. And after the body was covered with sand, people began to be aware that their world had become wider, their ideas larger, and their perspectives deeper. The present indeed held promises for the future. This became clear when, a few months later, many more students made plans to continue what their friend had begun.

So celebrating means the affirmation of the present, which becomes fully possible only by remembering the past and expecting more to come in the future. But celebrating in this sense very seldom takes place. Nothing is as difficult as really accepting one's own life. More often than not the present is denied, the past becomes a source of complaints, and the future is looked upon as a reason for despair or apathy.

When Jesus came to redeem humanity, He came to free us from the boundaries of time. Through Him it became clear not only that God is with us wherever our presence is in time or space, but also that our past does not have to be forgotten or denied but can be remembered and forgiven, and that we are still waiting for Him to come back and reveal to us what remains unseen. When Jesus left his Apostles, He gave them bread and wine in memory of what He did so that He could stay in their presence until the moment of His return. The word "Eucharist," which means thanksgiving, expresses a way of accepting life in which the past and the future are brought together in the present moment. This thanksgiving is meant to be a way of living that makes it possible to really celebrate life. Frequently, this Eucharistic celebration of life takes place elsewhere than where it is formally planned. Life is not always really celebrated where liturgies are held. Sometimes it is, but quite often it is not. Perhaps we have to become more sensitive to people and places where no one ever talks about liturgical reform or changes, but where life is fully affirmed in the deepest Eucharistic sense.

II. What Kind of Person Helps Us to Celebrate?

When we now wish to speak about the minister who enables us to celebrate, we are faced with the fact that, for someone in our culture, celebrating has become an extremely difficult thing to do. It seems that the Christian invitation to celebrate, to accept your life as the only life you have, to live it and accept it as good, has perhaps become the most difficult challenge we are facing at present.

We live in a culture in which these words of Jesus: "Do not worry about tomorrow, tomorrow will take care of itself" (Matthew 6:34), sound beautiful and romantic, but completely unrealistic. We live in such a utilitarian society that even our most intimate moments have become subject to the question: "What is the purpose of it?"

Today we do not just eat and drink; we have business lunches and fund-raising dinners. We do not just go horseback riding or swimming; we also invite our companions to do a little business on horseback or even in the pool. We do not just exercise our bodies or listen to beautiful songs, but we are also involved in a tremendous industry of sports and music. And we always keep on believing that the real thing is going to happen tomorrow. In this kind of life, the past has degenerated into a series of used or misused opportunities, the present into a constant concern about accomplishments, and the future into a make-believe paradise where we hope to finally receive what we always wanted but the existence of which we basically doubt.

A life like this cannot be celebrated, because we are constantly concerned with changing it into something else, always trying to do something to it, get something out of it, and make it fit our many plans and projects. We go to meetings, conferences, and congresses. We critically evaluate our part, discuss how to do it better in the future, and worry whether or not our great design will ever work out.

Our culture is a working, hurrying, and worrying culture with many opportunities but very little opportunity to celebrate life.

Insofar as this is true, we wonder how Christian our culture really is. It is a remarkable fact that the first and strongest reactions against this style of life have not come from the churches but from the many people living on the fringes of our society trying to give shape to what Theodore Roszak has called "the counter-culture." It is in the youthful opposition against our technocratic society that we truly find some authentic elements of a celebrating style of life. In the voices of those who announce the new counter-culture, we might hear sounds familiar to the Christian ear.

Roszak writes:

The primary project of our counter-culture is: to proclaim a new heaven and a new earth, so vast, so marvelous, that the inordinate claims of technical expertise must of necessity withdraw in the presence of such splendor to a subordinate and marginal status in the lives of man—we must be prepared to consider the scandalous possibility that wherever the visionary imagination grows bright, magic, that old antagonist of science, renews itself, transmitting our workday reality into something bigger, perhaps more frightening, certainly more adventurous than the lesser rationality of objective conscience can ever countenance. (*The Making of a Counter-Culture*, Anchor Books, Doubleday, New York, 1969, p. 240.)

This is announcing a new life that can be celebrated. But where does this leave ministers and priests who, though still having many faithful people in their churches, nonetheless do not find members of the counter-culture in their audiences? As long as ministers do no more than use Sunday to soften the pains of the week, our teaching, preaching, counseling, and organizing remain services to a life that cannot be celebrated.

But if we want to show the way to celebration, we have to become a special kind of person. We have to be and become more and more obedient—that is, we have to allow ourselves to be guided by the voices we hear. We have to be obedient to the voices of nature, to the voices of people, and to the voice of God.

Let us therefore look at the spirituality of the celebrant in the perspective of obedience.

1. OBEDIENCE TO THE VOICES OF NATURE

We who want to help others to celebrate have first of all to be obedient to the voices of nature and able to translate their message for others. Perhaps we have a lot to learn from the Native Americans here. It seems that we have become so concerned with mastering nature that we have become deaf to the voices of the rivers, the trees, the birds, and the flowers, which are constantly telling us about our own condition of life, our beauty, and our mortality.

A Wintu elder says:

The white people never cared for land or deer or bear. When we Indians kill meat, we eat it all up. When we dig roots, we make little holes . . . We shake down acorns and pine nuts. We don't chop down trees. We only use dead wood. But the white people plow up the ground, pull up the trees, kill everything. The tree says, "Don't, I am sore. Don't hurt me." But they chop it down and cut it up. The spirit of the land hates them . . . The Indians never hurt anything, but the white people destroy all. (op. cit., p. 245.)

The Native Americans know that they have to become more and more a part of nature, brother and sister of all creatures, so that we humans can find our real place in this world. They make their artwork in obedience to nature. In their masks, human and animal faces merge; in their pottery they use vegetables, such as the gourd, for models. It is nature that teaches them the forms they can make with their own hands.

It is not so difficult to understand why, through all the ages, people searching for the meaning of life tried to live as close to nature as possible. This includes not only St. Benedict, St. Francis, and St. Bruno in the olden days, but also Thomas

Merton, who lived in the woods of Kentucky, and the Benedictine monks, who built their monastery in an isolated canyon in New Mexico. It is not so strange that many young people are leaving the cities and going out into the country to find peace by listening to the voices of nature. And nature indeed speaks: the birds to St. Francis, the trees to the Native Americans, the river to Siddhartha. And the closer we come to nature, the closer we touch the core of life when we celebrate. Nature makes us aware of the preciousness of life. Nature tells us that life is precious not only because it is, but also because it does not have to be.

I remember sitting day after day at the same table in a dull restaurant where I had to eat my lunch. There was a beautiful red rose in a small vase in the middle of the table. I looked at the rose with sympathy and enjoyed its beauty. Every day I talked with my rose. But then I became suspicious. Because while my mood was changing during the week from happy to sad, from disappointed to angry, from energetic to apathetic, my rose was always the same. And moved by my suspicion I lifted my fingers to the rose and touched it. It was a plastic thing. I was deeply offended and never went back there to eat.

We cannot talk with plastic nature because it cannot tell us the real story about life and death. But if we are sensitive to the voice of nature, we might be able to hear sounds from a world where humanity and nature both find their shape. We will never fully understand the meaning of the sacramental signs of bread and wine when they do not make us realize that the whole of nature is a sacrament pointing to a reality far beyond nature itself. The presence of Christ in the Eucharist becomes a "special problem" only when we have lost our sense of His presence in all that is, grows, lives, and dies. What hap-

pens during a Sunday celebration can only be a real celebration when it reminds us in the fullest sense of what continu-
ally happens every day in the world that surrounds us. Bread
is more than bread; wine is more than wine: it is God with
us—not as an isolated event once a week but as the concentration of a mystery about which all of nature speaks day and
night.

Therefore, wasting food is not just a sin because there are
still so many hungry people in this world. It is a sin because
it is an offense against the sacramental reality of all we eat
and drink. But if we become more and more aware of the
voices of all that surrounds us and grow in respect and reverence for nature, then we will also be able to truly care for
humanity, which is embedded in nature like a sapphire in a
golden ring.

2. OBEDIENCE TO THE VOICES OF PEOPLE

For someone who wants to bring others to the celebration
of their lives, however, obedience to other people is even
more important than obedience to nature. Those who are really able to listen to other people will be able to recognize
their desire to celebrate as well as their fear of celebrating.
Celebration asks for the willingness to be enraptured by the
greatness of the mystery that surrounds us, and for many, who
would like to be in real touch with the ground of our own existence, there is a deep-seated anxiety about being absorbed by
it and losing our identity. We cannot live without the sun, but
we know that by coming too close to it we will be burned.
Our utilitarian tendencies have built a thick wall between us
and the source of our existence out of fear of total absorption.
But that same wall dooms us to live a cold and alienated life.
We know this, and so we desperately ask the minister, who

should know how to be close without being absorbed, to offer a way to participate in what is real life.

Roszak expresses this deep human desire when he writes:

> It is, at last, reality itself that must be participated in, must
> be seen, touched, breathed with the conviction that here is
> the ultimate ground of our existence, available to all, capa-
> ble of ennobling by its majesty the life of every man who
> opens himself. It is participation of this order—experiential
> and not merely political—that alone can guarantee the dig-
> nity and autonomy of the individual citizen. The strange
> youngsters who don cowbells and primitive talismans and
> who take to the public parks or wilderness to improvise
> outlandish communal ceremonies are in reality seeking to
> ground democracy safely beyond the culture of expertise.
> (op. cit., p. 265.)

But what many young people do is, in fact, part of the desire of everyone: to live life to the fullest, on the deepest possible level. Ministers and priests are challenged to offer the
way. They are looked upon as having a closer contact with this
reality than do many others, not as a personal privilege but as
a peculiar gift that they are to share with others. When
Roszak describes the shaman, he describes at the same time
the service that every minister and priest should offer: to be
like an "artist, who lays his work before the community in the
hope that through it, as through a window, the reality he has
fathomed can be witnessed by all who give attention" (op. cit.,
p. 260).

By participating in ritual, the community is able to see, feel,
touch, and fully experience without fear of absorption the reality that the minister has discovered for them. In Roszak's

words: "Ritual is the [minister's] way of broadcasting his vision, it is his instructive offering. If the [minister's] work is successful, the community's sense of reality will become expansive" (op. cit., p. 260). The great temptation is to consider the priest's or minister's closeness to the mystery of God as a privilege instead of a responsibility, and to turn one's own vocation into a special status and one's own ministry into an exploitive enterprise. But when ministers can really be obedient to their people, these same people will recognize their deep desire to see what their ministers have seen, to hear what their ministers have heard, to touch what their ministers have touched, and to break down the wall that separates them from the "Unseen Reality" (William James) of the universe. Then ministers will keep searching for ways and channels; forms and rituals; songs, dances, and gestures that enable others to come into vibrant contact with the Holy without fear. The ministers will make it possible for their people to take down their scaffolding and to freely celebrate life.

3. OBEDIENCE TO THE VOICE OF GOD

But do priests and ministers have any peculiar gift that they can share? Do they have a vision they can offer to help others see? Are they any closer than anyone else to the source of their existence, and do they know, feel, and see more deeply the condition in which their people are imprisoned but from which they want to become free?

If the answer is No, we may rightly wonder if ministers will ever be able to help others celebrate life. Those who are set apart to lead people to the heart of God's mystery will never be able to do so when they themselves are blind, do not know the way, or are afraid to approach the throne of God.

Ordination means the recognition and affirmation of the

fact that a person has gone beyond the walls of fear, lives in intimate contact with God of the living, and has a burning desire to show others the way to God. Ordination does not make anybody anything but is the solemn recognition of the fact that someone has been able to be obedient to God, to hear God's voice and understand God's call, and that this person can offer others the way to that same experience. Therefore, ministers who want to make celebration possible must be people of prayer. Only people of prayer can lead others to celebration, because everyone who comes into contact with such people realizes that they draw their powers from a source that cannot be easily located but that is strong and deep. The freedom that gives ministers a certain independence is not authoritarian or distant. Rather, it makes them rise above the immediate needs and most urgent desires of the people around them. They are deeply moved by things happening near them, but they do not allow themselves to be crushed by them. They listen attentively, speak with a self-evident authority, but do not easily become excited or nervous. In all that they say or do, ministers prove to have a vision that guides their lives. To that vision they are obedient. It makes them distinguish sharply between what is important and what is not. Ministers are not insensitive to what excites people, but they evaluate their needs differently by seeing them in the perspective of their vision. They are happy and content when people listen, but they do not want to form cliques. They do not attach themselves to anybody exclusively. What they say sounds convincing and obvious, but they do not force their opinions on anybody and are not irritated when people do not accept their ideas or do not fulfill their wishes. All this shows that the vision of the minister is what counts and that the minister should strive to make this vision a reality.

But ministers also have an inner freedom in respect to this ideal. They know they will not see their purposes realized, and they should consider themselves only as guides to it. They are impressively free toward their own life. From their actions it becomes clear that they consider their own existence of secondary importance. They do not live to keep themselves alive but to build a new world of which they have already seen the first images and which is so appealing that the borderline between life and death loses its definitiveness. Ministers not only celebrate life but can also make others desire to do the same.

And so we have seen how obedience to nature, to people, and to God are three characteristics of ministers who want to be servants in the celebration of life. None of us can claim for ourselves to be such a celebrant. Only Jesus could, because only He was obedient to God and creation unto death, even death on the Cross. It is on the Cross that He became the celebrant of life in the full sense, because it was there that death was conquered and life regained in the total act of obedience. In this way, any of us who call ourselves ministers can only consider ourselves to be weak reflections of Him who gave His life on the Cross and made it available to all who are called to celebrate their lives as children of the same Father.

Conclusion

The main idea of this chapter is that obedience to God and creation is the basic condition for being a celebrant of life. If ministers claim to want others to fully accept their lives as their own by affirmation, remembrance, and expectation, they themselves are challenged to be servants of life who can listen to the voices of nature, people, and God and announce what they have heard to those who want to join in the act of celebration.

Through celebration we enter into the Kingdom of Heaven. But Jesus said: "Unless you change and become like little children you will never enter the Kingdom of Heaven" (Matthew 18:3). It is through childlike obedience that life becomes a way to the Kingdom. And if you have ever offered bread and wine to God on the rim of the Grand Canyon, you might have then experienced that we can really celebrate when humility has made us free. We are only a very small part of history and have only one short life to live, but when we take the fruits of our labor in our hands and stretch our arms to God in the deep belief that God hears us and accepts our gifts, then we know that all of our life is given, and given to celebrate.

A Spirituality of Ministry

If there is any sentence in the Gospel that expresses in a very concentrated way everything I have tried to say in the five chapters of this book, it is the sentence spoken by Jesus to His Apostles the day before His death: "A man can have no greater love than to lay down his life for his friends" (John 15:13).

For me these words summarize the meaning of all Christian ministry. If teaching, preaching, individual pastoral care, organizing, and celebrating are acts of service that go beyond the level of professional expertise, it is precisely because in these acts ministers are asked to lay down their own lives for their friends. There are many people who, through long training, have reached a high level of competence in terms of the understanding of human behavior, but there are few who are willing to lay down their lives for others and make their weakness a source of creativity. For many individuals, professional training means power. But ministers, who take off their clothes to wash the feet of their friends, are powerless, and their training and formation are meant to enable them to face their own weakness without fear and make it available to others. It is exactly this creative weakness that gives the ministry its momentum.

Teaching becomes ministry when teachers move beyond the transference of knowledge and are willing to offer their own life-experience to their students so that paralyzing anxiety can be removed, new liberating insight can come about, and real learning can take place. Preaching becomes ministry when preachers move beyond the "telling of the story" and make their own deepest selves available to their listeners so that they will be able to receive the Word of God. Individual care becomes ministry when those who want to be of help move beyond the careful balance of give and take with a willingness to risk their own lives and remain faithful to their suffering brothers and sisters, even when this endangers their own name and fame. Organizing becomes ministry when organizers move beyond their desire for concrete results and look at the world with the unwavering hope for a total renewal. Celebrating becomes ministry when celebrants move beyond the limits of protective rituals to an obedient acceptance of life as a gift.

Although none of these tasks of service can ever be fulfilled without careful preparation and proved competence, none can ever be called ministry when this competence is not grounded in the radical commitment to lay down one's own life in the service of others. Ministry means the ongoing attempt to put one's own search for God, with all the moments of pain and joy, despair and hope, at the disposal of those who want to join this search but do not know how. Therefore, ministry in no way is a privilege. Instead, it is the core of the Christian life. No Christian is a Christian without being a minister. There are many more forms of ministry than the five I have discussed in this book, which usually fill the daily life of the ordained minister and priest. But whatever form the Christian ministry takes, the basis is always the same: to lay down one's life for one's friends.

But why do people lay down their lives for their friends? There is only one answer to that question: to give new life. All functions of the ministry are life-giving. Whether one teaches, preaches, counsels, plans, or celebrates, the aim is always to open new perspectives, to offer new insight, to give new strength, to break the chains of death and destruction, and to create new life which can be affirmed. In short, to make one's own weakness creative.

So, if a man wants to be a minister, let him be happy to make his weaknesses his special boast so that the power of Christ may stay over him . . . for when he is weak then he is strong (cf. St. Paul, 2 Corinthians 12:9–10).

But although no one can live and keep living without need for this ministry, it seems that for many people, who are exposed to the growing destructive potentials of our world and have seen the most ruthless and cruel annihilation of life during their own short history, Christianity does not seem able to offer this indispensable ministry. When they hear about the life of Jesus and His Apostles, they wonder what that story has to do with this age of atomic power. When they are told that their lives play a meaningful role in the great history of mankind, in which the redemption through the death of Christ has to become more and more visible, they, in fact, do not see much more than an increasing escalation of war, poverty, cruelty, and senseless destruction of their environment. When they are comforted with the idea that this life is not final and that they will find its continuation in a world after this, their question is whether there is much here that calls for continuation and whether it makes sense to think about some new life in a vague future when even words like "tomorrow," "next week," "next year," and "later" are losing their meaning in a world that can kill not only us but also our history.

Perhaps the apparent crisis in the Christian ministry is directly related to the fact that in the modern age, we are exposed to so many fearful and widely contrasting experiences and ideas that we hardly have any meaningful roots in the past nor much expectation for the future. Robert Jay Lifton speaks of a "worldwide sense of . . . historical dislocation," which he describes as a "break in the sense of connection which men have long felt with the vital and nourishing symbols of their cultural tradition—symbols revolving around family, idea systems, religion, and the life cycle in general." ("Protean Man," *Partisan Review,* 1968, p.16.)

But if our atomic age—which is able to destroy not just individuals and families but whole cultures and their histories, whole countries and their chances for rebirth—has caused many people to lose confidence in the Christian ministry, the question is whether we have fully understood what it means today to lay down one's life for one's friends.

Maybe we have to look beyond the institutional church to grasp the full implications of this call, because words such as "concentration," "meditation," and "contemplation" are again used today with great reverence by thousands of young people who will never think of going to a church or consulting a Christian minister. In a great variety of ways, they try to break through their confusion and restlessness to find in the center of their own experience something that can make them reach beyond their own limited consciousness. They are experimenting with new methods of relating to each other, new ways of nonviolent communication, new approaches to the experience of oneness and union, new means of mutual care, and new attempts to celebrate their lives. They borrow symbols not only from Christian tradition but also from Buddhism and Hinduism; they try to broaden their sensitivities by natural and artificial stimuli such as drugs and alcohol. They read, sing, and prophesy to experience a new sense of freedom.

It is no exaggeration to say that, while the churches become emptier year after year, new forms of ministry are being sought on the periphery of Christianity, and that teaching, preaching, caring, planning, and celebrating are appearing in new ways in the catacombs of our modern cities. In the middle of our chaotic world we have become increasingly aware of the permanent threat of total destruction and cry desperately for a new "spirituality" that enables the human race to come to terms with its search for meaning. This new spirituality is described by Lifton as "the path of experiential transcendence—of seeking a sense of immortality in the way the mystics always have, through psychic experiences of such great intensity that time and death are, in effect, eliminated" (op. cit., p. 27).

It is painful to realize that very few ministers are able to offer the rich mystical tradition of Christianity as a source of rebirth for the generation searching for new life in the midst of the debris of a faltering civilization. Perhaps our self-consciousness, fear of rejection, and preoccupation with church quarrels prevent us from being free to experience the transcendent Spirit of God, which can renew our hearts and our world as well. Perhaps we are not ready yet to give the so-much-needed guidance to the thousands who engage themselves in a risky experimentation with the powers of the unseen. Perhaps we ourselves have lost contact with these powers and can only qualify the stories of the catacombs as weird, dangerous, and signs of immaturity. But I am afraid that the many obvious mistakes, failures, and unintelligible experiments blind us to the fact that underneath all of this there is a deep desire for new insight, new understanding, and most of all, new life.

If I can trust my own feelings and limited experiences with young students, it seems that we are approaching a period of an increased search for spirituality that is the experience of God in this very moment of our existence. When there is so little in the past to hold on to and so little in the future to look forward to, the reality that can give meaning to one's life must be experienced here and now.

A twenty-year-old Catholic student, who considered his church completely irrelevant to his needs but who was desperately searching for meaning in his life, said to me: "We tried drugs and it didn't work; we tried sex and it didn't work; the next thing will be suicide—in the coming years you will see the number of suicides skyrocketing." The only possible response to this seems to be to rediscover the transcending power of the spiritual life by which we are able to stand strong even when surrounded by shifting ideologies; crumbling political, social, and religious structures; and a constant threat of war and total destruction. It may be extremely difficult for us in the modern age to feel close to Jesus of Nazareth, who lived in another world; it may be even more difficult to look forward to the day of His return; but more than ever it may be possible to experience the Spirit of Christ as a living Spirit who makes it possible to break through the boundaries of our imprisoned existence and makes us free to work for a new world.

But this way of the transcendental experience is a way that requires ministry. It calls for men and women who do not shy away from careful preparation, solid formation, and qualified training, but who at the same time are free enough to break through the restrictive boundaries of disciplines and specialties in the conviction that the Spirit moves beyond professional expertise. It calls for Christians who are willing to develop their sensitivity to God's presence in their own lives, as well as in the lives of others, and to offer their experiences as a way of recognition and liberation to other human beings. It calls for ministers in the true sense, who lay down their own lives for their friends, helping them to distinguish between the constructive and the destructive spirits and making them free for the discovery of God's life-giving Spirit in the midst of this maddening world. It calls for creative weakness.

Epilogue

When I look back at the way I wrote this book, I begin to realize that it is a very personal book. In fact, it is an attempt to articulate ideas and feelings about the ministry based on the ups and downs of my own experiences. I hoped that a careful reflection on these experiences could throw some light on the different questions I had asked myself and give some insight into the direction I want to go from here.

I also hoped that my "confession" could be of some help to others in the ongoing discussion about the value and meaning of the Christian ministry. Therefore, the conclusion of this book does not want to suggest the end of a discussion but the beginning of one. In fact, this discussion has already become part of this book, because while presenting the different chapters to priests and ministers, to sisters and social workers, to parents and students, I became more and more aware that many people had completely different experiences from those I had and could hardly recognize themselves in the ideas I tried to formulate. When I was confronted with so many questions and criticisms, my first inclination was to go back to the text and start all over again. But then I realized that this was impossible, because I could not change my own past and had to accept the limitation attached to being personal. My friend Don McNeill even made me see that it would be much more realistic and in line with my own conviction if I presented the questions and criticisms at the end of this book instead of smuggling the untested answers into the text itself.

Well, there are many unanswered questions. And every chapter has its own. I should like to formulate some of them here.

ON TEACHING

What you say about the relationship between student and teacher may be interesting for a college situation, but what about grade school and high school? Does your whole idea not become very romantic when you are confronted with the task of teaching mathematics to small children who can hardly sit quiet for a minute?

ON PREACHING

Don't you have to be a trained psychologist to be available to others in the way you suggest? What about the ordinary minister who has to get up into that pulpit every week? Aren't you a little too demanding? And, after all, isn't the direct presentation of the Word of God, welcome or unwelcome, more important than the subtle clarification of people's feelings?

ON INDIVIDUAL PASTORAL CARE

I work as a chaplain in a prison with twenty men in one cell. When I come into the cell the prisoners fight for the chance to talk with me and to ask me for very concrete help— to find out where their children are, to visit their wives, to ask when their trials will be, to get some medicine, et cetera. What does it mean to be a pastor for these particular individuals? It seems that I don't have to go beyond professionalism to fulfill the task of four different professions at once!

ON ORGANIZING

If you had been a priest in the ghettos, you never would have said what you did. You missed the point completely. You are simply soft-pedaling the whole issue. You suggest an unrealistic detachment in an emergency situation.

ON CELEBRATING

What about the children who have never lived in nature and probably never will? What about the millions of people living in the ever-growing cities? How should they celebrate?

I do not know the answers to these questions and criticisms. They are undoubtedly a convincing illustration of the limitations of my own ideas. But I hope that they also show the value and necessity of the sharing of experiences as a primary condition for an ongoing search for a spirituality of ministry.

About the Author

© Neal McDonough

HENRI J. M. NOUWEN was a Catholic priest who taught at several theological institutes and universities in his home country of the Netherlands and in the United States. He shared the final years of his life with people with mental and physical disabilities at L'Arche Daybreak Community in Toronto, Canada. He died in 1996. Father Nouwen authored many books on the spiritual life, including *Reaching Out, The Wounded Healer, The Return of the Prodigal Son,* and *The Inner Voice of Love.*

Visit www.nouwen.net to learn more about Henri Nouwen or e-mail nouwencentre@nouwen.net.